P9-DGY-210

TWENTIETH CENTURY INTERPRETATIONS
OF

THE PLAYBOY OF THE WESTERN WORLD

A Collection of Critical Essays

Edited by

THOMAS R. WHITAKER

Prentice-Hall, Inc. 

Englewood Cliffs, N. J.

 Library of Congress Catalog Card Number 69–17369. Printed in the United States of America.

Current printing (last number):
10 9 8 7 6 5 4 3 2 1

Prentice-Hall International, Inc. (*London*)

Contents

Introduction: On Playing with *The Playboy**

by Thomas R. Whitaker

I

For more than sixty years now the western world (in a larger sense than Pegeen Mike knew she intended) has been delightedly responding to John Millington Synge's invitation to join him in an exuberant, astringent, and self-illuminating theatrical playfulness. Of course, that invitation has sometimes been rudely turned down: most notably in Dublin during the turbulent week of January, 1907, when *The Playboy of the Western World* was first produced, and again in New York and Philadelphia during the winter of 1911–12, when the Irish Players had to cope first with riotous audiences and then with the arrest of the entire cast. The Philadelphia liquor-dealer who brought charges had stayed in the theater, according to Lady Gregory,

> only till Shawneen's "coat of a Christian man" was left in Michael James's hands. He made a disturbance then and was turned out, but was able to find as much indecency even in that conversation as would demoralise a monastery. His brother, a priest, had stayed all through, and found we had committed every sin mentioned in the Act.

Those early rejections of *The Playboy* claimed to be not only moral and religious but also political. Arthur Griffith's *United Irish-*

* I want to thank Donald McClelland, who helped me look into the history of *The Playboy*'s performances, and Ann Saddlemyer, who kindly offered to let me read the Appendix to the Oxford edition of *The Playboy* in advance of its publication.

man, the New York *Gaelic American,* and such societies as the Clan-na-Gael were able to whip up an indignation that depended in part upon the touchy sensibilities of an aggrieved nationalism. As George Bernard Shaw put it, the Clan-na-Gael hit upon

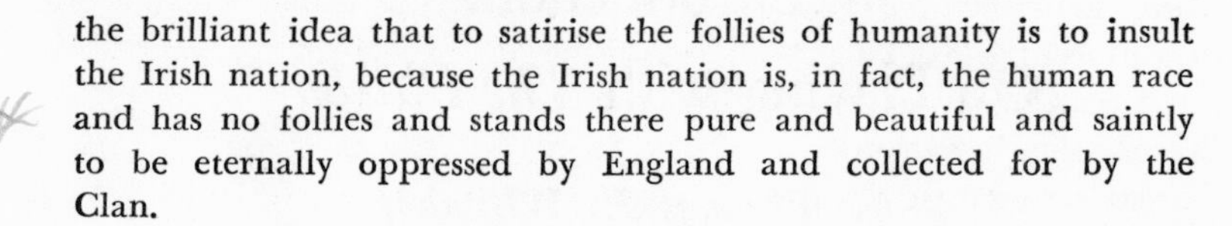

> the brilliant idea that to satirise the follies of humanity is to insult the Irish nation, because the Irish nation is, in fact, the human race and has no follies and stands there pure and beautiful and saintly to be eternally oppressed by England and collected for by the Clan.

Shaw was unfair, as usual, but right. We all traffic in such brilliant ideas, though sometimes we think our purity destined not to be eternally oppressed but to impose its own will upon the western world. "By the will of God," we say with Michael James, "we'll have peace now for our drinks."

An ironic recalling of the moral, religious, or political attacks upon *The Playboy,* however, does not take us far toward understanding what it means to reject Synge's invitation. William Butler Yeats made the necessary point when he declared: "The outcry against *The Playboy* was an outcry against its style, against its way of seeing." And that way of seeing, as I have hinted, encompasses its own opposition. If we refuse to discover ourselves in the play's comic protagonist, who is both victim and victor, and if we also refuse to discover ourselves in the vicariously rebellious but anxiously closed society which longs for that protagonist, half-creates him, celebrates him, and then casts him out—we merely make a scapegoat of the play itself. And the play knows why. Not for nothing is Christy Mahon a potato-digging poet, ostensible father-murderer, seeming savior, lord of misrule, and consequent scapegoat. He is a richly symbolic man.

Many implications of *The Playboy*'s remarkably self-aware style are spelled out (from various points of view and with some illuminating disagreements) in the essays that I have included in this collection. W. B. Yeats, who may well remain Synge's most profound commentator, describes the milieu upon which *The Playboy* made its first impact and assesses the qualities of Synge's style. Una Ellis-Fermor writes of Synge's paradoxical fusion of dramatic power and Irish nature-poetry. And Cyril Cusack, drawing upon his experience in the role of Christy Mahon, discusses that tension between naturalism and theatrical fantasy which is one of the play's enigmatic virtues. The next four essays provide a more sustained focus upon *The Playboy* itself: T. R. Henn presents "several sides" of its richly ironic structure; Norman Podhoretz and Patricia Meyer Spacks look in different ways at the social and psychological paradoxes related to Christy as self-constructed hero; and Howard Pearce redresses the balance by warning us that the play does not take Christy's romantic apotheosis without irony. The excerpted "View Points" round out this critical conversation: David Greene retraces something of Synge's process of enriching and sharpening the play's structure and diction; Ronald Peacock considers the ironic edge given to its "fine language"; Herbert Howarth defines the "surreality" of its world and notes some of its theatrical qualities; and J. L. Styan shows how the style controls our imaginative responses in the theater as Synge engages us with an extravagant but subtle playfulness.

What remains to be said? I doubt that we will reject *The Playboy* out of moral indignation in a day when we applaud *Endgame* or *The Balcony*. Perhaps the danger now is that we may condescend to Synge. We may "place" him at a comfortable distance and respond to *The Playboy* with the secure delight appropriate to an acknowledged "masterpiece of the Irish dramatic movement." Ronald Peacock has claimed that Synge "looked backward, not forward." T. S. Eliot and others have said that his poetic language is too idiosyncratic to provide a foundation for later playwrights. Richard Hayes has called Synge "a great dramatist whose work has extended neither the sensibility, subject matter, nor form of the English theater."

Is *The Playboy* a splendid dead-end? We should at least recognize (as T. R. Henn, Richard Ellmann, Herbert Howarth, and others have made clear) that Synge's sensibility had a great impact upon the work of Yeats and of James Joyce. We should also recognize, I think, his somewhat less definite links with later Irish dramatists skilled in counterpointing lyricism and irony, laughter and violence, trenchant talk and collapsing action: Sean O'Casey, Denis Johnston, Samuel Beckett. (And that is to say nothing about such lesser matters as Eugene O'Neill's attempts to imitate Synge's language or William Faulkner's assimilation of his cadences: ". . . and he leaning on it motionless in the hot shimmer of the sun.")

But I think it more important now to suggest another way—less simply a matter of "influence"—in which Synge relates to our time. Cusack has said that in Paris, at the First International Theatre Festival in 1954, *The Playboy* "found its true home and audience." Of course, the play had long since reached Paris in translation: in 1914 Lugné-Poë directed *Le Baladin du Monde Occidental* at the Theatre de l'Oeuvre. (Barrett Clark thought it farther from the original than the Künstlertheater production of *Der Held des Westerlands* that he had seen in Munich.) But Cusack rightly suggests that *The Playboy* is genuinely *of* our larger western world. "The striking feature of modern art," Thomas Mann has said, "is that it has ceased to recognize the categories of tragic and comic, or the dramatic classifications, tragedy and comedy. It sees life as tragicomedy, with the result that the grotesque is its most genuine style . . ." And Synge's masterpiece in the grotesque style is also the play in which he most fully engages what seems the obsessive subject of modern drama: life as a question of "role-playing." It is true that drama has long used disguises, plays-within-plays, and other metaphorical gestures integral to the medium; it has long seen life as this great stage, where each man plays many parts. But during the past century or so, drama has become (like other manifestations of modern consciousness) yet more ironically self-reflexive and more skeptical of postulated essences. Life has seemed to become more inescapably and incongruously histrionic. The strutting and fretting have become more grotesque.

Synge may not have known Arthur Schnitzler's *The Green Cockatoo,* where "reality passes into play, play into reality," and where a Paris café is described in terms applicable to his Mayo pub: "This is a strange place. People who play criminals come here—and others who are criminals without suspecting it." And Synge did not live to read the words that Hugo von Hofmannsthal gave to a player in his "Prologue to Brecht's *Baal*": "The actor is the amoeba among all living things and therefore he is the symbolic man. The amoeba, that indeterminate primitive creature, which lets the situation dictate whether it should be animal or plant." But because *The Playboy* develops similar insights, Synge's understanding of the histrionic must be placed in the context of dramatists from Ibsen to Genet who have been haunted by these implications of their medium.

II

Stripped of its qualifying ironies, *The Playboy* presents a remarkable parabolic action. The shy and lonely farm-boy threatened by an Oedipal fate (a forced marriage with the widow who "did suckle me for six weeks when I came into the world") has erupted in panicky violence against the father whom he fears. Now, finding himself among those who shelter him and draw his story from him, he gradually lends himself (with a childlike creative faith) to the role of glorious parricide—whereupon, through the ups and downs of exploratory prevarication, he discovers his poetic power, his ability to love and be loved, his strength and courage. After surviving the appropriate ordeals (exposure as a liar, confrontation with the repeatedly resurrected old Mahon, rejection by society as a murderer), Christy leaves the stage a new man, independent and reconciled with the father—indeed, having gaily swapped places with him. Though calling himself "master of all fights from now," he no longer seems tempted to maintain an insecure ego by violence and deceit. In fact, he now invokes blessings upon those (including his once-beloved Pegeen) who had seemed fools or worse a moment before: in their adulation and their rejection they have made him "a likely gaffer in the end of all." The "playboy" as hoaxer has become the "playboy" as genuine champion, beyond their understanding—though not beyond Pegeen's belated longing. Role-playing has led to the authentic; lies have led to truth.

Or so it seems—for such an interpretation contains difficulties. Una Ellis-Fermor has said that whether this finale is Christy's "self-realization, as he thinks, or the expansion of a superb fantasy, as we half-suppose, matters little." But Howard Pearce holds that it matters very much, and that the play drastically qualifies Christy's romantic vision. Cyril Cusack, perhaps still weighting the play's naturalism more heavily than its theatricalism, thinks the finale weak because a "void," the artist's "flight from reality," has become the resolution. And Mrs. Spacks, who sees the "man" and the "pose" as finally identical in Christy, suggests that language comes to control him as much as he comes to control language. Surely we must then ask: Has Christy's kind of playing really led him to the actual? Or has Synge's kind of playing led *us* from the actual into the realm of myth? Or has the entire play enabled us to participate in both possibilities? And if so, how are those possibilities related to one another?

The Playboy locates itself in a much-disputed territory: the "educational" function of role-playing in "life" and in "art." The play's very ambivalences, I think, are clues to its meaning. Its grotesque style elicits from us an unusually sustained combination of spontaneous sympathy and detached irony. We share in Christy's passionate improvisation and in the formal patterns of Synge's precise comic control. Located both "inside" and "outside" Christy, we follow the reciprocal process of his self-construction and self-discovery. And in assessing that process, we share Synge's marvellously balanced awareness of the wry fictiveness of the seeming actual and the potent actuality of our most profound fictions. But these effects all point to the central mysteries of drama itself. For drama is that art of cooperative role-playing which submits passionate improvisation and its spontaneously doubled response in the spectator to formal control, locates us both "inside" and "outside" the action, and so brings to immediate awareness much that otherwise remains hidden in the more compulsively histrionic texture of our lives. Such art leads us through self-constructions to self-discoveries. *The Playboy,* then, is "about" both the drama of life and the life of drama. It invites us to focus the self-blinding and self-illuminating possibilities of our shared histrionic sensibility. In that way, the play transcends the ambiguities of its central parable. Its role-playing does lead us to the authentic.

But before looking at how the detailed structure of *The Playboy* develops that meaning, I want to relate the histrionic Christy Mahon to John Synge—and Synge to some other playwrights. Most striking, at first glance, is the distance between the sometimes violent and frequently prevaricating Christy and Synge himself. John Butler Yeats, who called Christy "a young poet in the supreme difficulty of getting born," also said that "Synge was morally one of the most fastidious men I ever met," a "man of peace" whose conversation "had the charm of entire sincerity, a quality rare among men and artists." Synge's friend Stephen MacKenna, the translator of Plotinus, said that he never knew "a man with so passionate, so pedantic a value for truth as Synge. He didn't so much judge the lie intellectually or morally as simply hate it—as one hates a bad smell or a filthy taste." And John Masefield, on observing Synge at the first London performance of *The Playboy* in June of 1907, reflected "that he was the only person there sufficiently simple to be really interested in living people, and that it was this simplicity which gave him his charm."

That is impressive testimony, and it indicates how fully Synge had let go of our usual hypocrisy and evasive sophistication. "There is nothing so great and sacred as what is most simple in life," he could say—and we recall another master of the grotesque, Anton Chekhov, who said with his life as with his words: "The nearer a man is to truth, the more intelligent and simple he is." Such distance between the playwright's *persona* and his more evidently theatrical *dramatis personae* results partly from the fact that alertness to the histrionic may help us to avoid the more serious forms of self-hypnosis and self-closure. Chekhov's tragicomic rendering of theatrical lives in *The Sea Gull* or *The Cherry Orchard* is dedicated to the transcendence of our usual narcissistic role-playing. A similar paradox enters Ibsen's drama. Peer Gynt, an ancestor of Christy Mahon, works through the theatrical onion-skins of his life to confront his nothingness and the possibility of an new authenticity. *The Wild Duck,* unlike its sardonic and self-justifying Dr. Relling, does not prescribe "the life-lie" but invites us to engage in an alert and sympathetic playing of roles which are themselves constituted by a more defensive role-playing. We open ourselves to the meaning of the characters' self-closure. Quite similar is the strategy of Synge's *The Well of the Saints,* which does not celebrate Martin Doul's choice of blindness and self-delusion but leads us, through qualified sympathy with that choice, beyond the habitual blindness of those who think they see.

I don't mean in these remarks to underestimate the degree to which Synge's own moral *persona* was just that: a paradoxically anti-theatrical mask, a social role which in its quiet self-effacement enabled him to observe others undisturbed, and which did not exhaust his protean self. It seems clear that Synge's romanticism and exoticism provided a field for heuristic self-projection that compensated for the lack of active richness in his social role. Two early "imaginary portraits"—"Vita Vecchia" and "Étude Morbide" —indicates his understanding of romantic projection in art and life, as partly shaped by the styles of Huysmans, Pater, and Wilde. *The Aran Islands* and the later travel-sketches are informed by a much quieter and more profound awareness of how the natural scene and its inhabitants may focus and articulate the impulses of the observer's own depths. Implicit in the selection of event and the texture of the prose, that awareness sometimes becomes explicit—as in *The Aran Islands* when Synge remarks on the "affinity between the moods of these people and the moods of varying rapture and dismay that are frequent in artists, and in certain forms of alienation," or in "The Vagrants of Wicklow" when this young man who would die of cancer in a few years notes that "in moments when one is most aware of this ceaseless fading" of nature's beauty "some incident of tramp life gives a local human intensity to the shadow of one's mood"—and then without further comment describes his meeting with a tramp "suffering from some terrible disease."

In the plays Synge carried such self-projections further toward what we rather misleadingly call "dramatic objectivity"; that is, he increased their solidity, purged them of defensive and self-gratifying nuances, and opened them to our cooperative participation. *Riders to the Sea* focuses with a difficult simplicity the passions aroused by the overwhelming sense of death's immanence in life, and it enables us to follow them, with Maurya, to the point of acceptance beyond tragedy, all passion spent. *Deirdre of the Sorrows*—written after Synge's engagement to Molly Allgood and left uncompleted because of his own death—invites us to explore the gestures of another kind of heroic acceptance. And the four other plays allow Synge to engage his audiences with an aggressive but luminously therapeutic playfulness that the silently observant writer chose not to employ in his own person.

As Synge shaped those solid and translucent projections, he developed his distinctive speech. Based on the English of the West of Ireland (with its elements of Gaelic syntax and archaic English vocabulary), enriched by contact with the English Bible, Elizabethan plays, and Lady Gregory's *Cuchulain of Muirthemne*—"Your *Cuchulain*," Synge wrote her, "is a part of my daily bread"—it is above all a stage speech, condensed and refined through many drafts in accord with the heightened dynamic relations of the theater. Its own temptations are manifest: the mechanical lilt, the predictable lyric inflation, the too neatly sardonic counterpoint. But in Synge's best work its fluctuations of tone enact the dance of an alert consciousness responding to the total dramatic situation. The difficulties that such speech made for the Abbey players (about which Maire Nic Shiubhlaigh and W. G. Fay have commented) indicate not merely its distance from their everyday language and from "stage Irish" but also its demand for sustained alertness.

In such ways, I think, Synge moved as artist through a complex role-playing toward the authenticity of continually renewed openness. Christy Mahon, his seeming antithesis, was also his twin. W. B. Yeats clearly saw that dramatic and antithetical relation between Synge and his art; and though Yeats's comments partly derive from his own theory of the mask, he also learned from Synge's example. Many of Yeats's remarks about self-discovery through pursuit of one's opposite take on new light when we think of *The Playboy*. "If we cannot imagine ourselves as different from what we are and assume that second self," he said in 1909, "we cannot impose a discipline upon ourselves, though we may accept one from others. Active virtue as distinguished from passive acceptance of a current code is therefore theatrical, consciously dramatic." That same year, in "The Death of Synge," he said: "I think that all happiness depends on the energy to assume the mask of some other self; that all joyous or creative life is a re-birth as something not oneself, something which has no memory and is created in a moment and perpetually renewed." And it was in 1907, the year of *The Playboy*, that Yeats began to write *The Player Queen*, that tragedy which became a farce, about the fulfilment that comes with finding one's antithetical self. Yeats's Decima finds that self as she assumes the role of the Queen in expectation of imminent death. She is a cousin of Christy's—one of a number. Our minds are carried forward, past Luigi Pirandello's more sardonic study of related paradoxes in *Henry IV,* to Ugo Betti's *The Queen and the Rebels,* where the prostitute Argia discovers her true queenliness by a similarly bold role-playing, and on to Jean Genet's *The Balcony,* where Madame Irma with a darker irony assumes the role of Queen as she initiates us into the meaning of a skillful speeding toward absence.

The modern theater offers many playboys. Sometimes, as in Shaw's *Heartbreak House,* the role-playing seems to work in reverse: "In this house," says Hector Hushabye, "we know all the poses: our game is to find out the man under the pose." In Edward Albee's *Who's Afraid of Virginia Woolf?* the updated name of that game is "Get the Guests." Sometimes, as in Pirandello, Genet, or Beckett, the texture of self-conscious role-playing may seem to define a brothel of mirrors or the self's closed room. "Me—(*he yawns*) —to play," begins the Hamm of *Endgame,* who already knows more than Shaw's Hector about such matters. But sometimes, as in Betti or Bertolt Brecht in their different ways, the play recognizes that the histrionic sensibility can be both a trap and a means of self-understanding. We are then closer to Synge. Another cousin of Christy's is Azdak in Brecht's *The Caucasian Chalk Circle,* whose swift rise from cowardly intellectual to lord of misrule, scapegoat, and ironic judge depends partly upon his own learning through bold improvisation and partly upon the play's comic control of his relations to the triply-layered audience that learns through such role-playing. Not surprisingly, the next step for *The Playboy* after finding "its true home and audience" in Paris in 1954 was its entry into the repertory of the Berliner Ensemble in 1956, directed by Peter Palitzsch and Manfred Wekwerth.

In Synge's own time and language, Oscar Wilde had most boldly summed up romantic aesthetics with the skeptically histrionic accent that points toward such twentieth-century developments. "The first duty in life is to assume a pose," said Wilde; "what the second is, no one has yet found out." But Wilde understood his own ignorance more profoundly than that. He had a striking sense of the heuristic value of masks: their ability to release the mind from habitual fixations, to focus the impulses of the subliminal self, and to provide the forms through which we apprehend existence. Wilde's own elaborate playboy *persona* had little in common with the personal simplicity of John Synge. But when Synge was in France (according to Maurice Bourgeois) he persuaded a Breton friend to translate Wilde's *Intentions* and helped him with that project. Among the remarks in "The Decay of Lying" which foreshadow *The Playboy* is this: "Many a young man starts in life with a natural gift for exaggeration which, if nurtured in congenial and sympathetic surroundings, or by the imitation of the best models, might grow into something really great and wonderful."

Wilde's own most sparkling exercise in the theatrical use of social masks, *The Importance of Being Earnest,* he called a "trivial comedy for serious people." Despite great differences in milieu and imaginative range, Synge harked back to Wilde when, in the preface to *The Tinker's Wedding,* he said: "The drama is made serious—in the French sense of the word—not by the degree in which it is taken up with problems that are serious in themselves, but by the degree in which it gives the nourishment, not very easy to define, on which our imaginations live." What Synge meant by that nourishment—and it was richer, tougher, and more self-opening than anything to which Wilde committed himself—is clear in *The Playboy of the Western World.* There he dramatized his implicit understanding that the art of highest seriousness is a grotesque role-playing.

III

"All art is a collaboration," wrote Synge—and we may properly take that statement to refer to more than the process of composition. Synge's comments upon his personal participation in orchestral music (quoted in Ann Saddlemyer's study of his aesthetic theory) indicate how open he was to the collaborative dimensions of the art-work itself. The full meaning of *The Playboy*'s text begins to appear, I think, only when we try to read it as a "score" for a participatory event.

The Playboy's formal control of our cooperative role-playing attains that wholeness or many-sidedness which Synge equated with "sanity." It does so through a style that compresses into a single form all that Synge meant when he said: "it is only the catastrophes of life that give substance and power to the tragedy and humour which are the true poles of art." The larger structures of that grotesque style depend first of all upon a synthesis of comic convention and naturalism.

The *dramatis personae* descend from traditional types: the hero of New Comedy (modified in the direction of fool and braggart), the heroine (with a touch of Boucicault), the rival youth (a simpler and more effeminate fool), the two "heavy" fathers (each with his distinctive humor), the older woman who trades on her fading sexual attractiveness (worldly wise, a matchmaker, rival of the heroine), the two parasites (humorous and suspicious), and the peripheral group that represents society. The situations, too, are highly traditional: the hero's violence against the oppressive father, the complex love-rivalry (with suggestions of incest), the victory of the lord of misrule and his rejection as a scapegoat, the torture of the tricky slave, the resurrection of the old man (as adversary and as rescuing agent), the reconciliation of son and father, and the final transcendence of the closed society. Mrs. Spacks has pointed to the folktale for analogies to the strange action of this play, but one might also point to comic tradition. Indeed, one could almost fit the play into Northrop Frye's *Anatomy of Criticism* as a complex instance of the second or "quixotic phase" of comedy, where a society is formed by or around the hero but cannot sustain itself. The hero, Frye remarks, "is usually himself at least partly a comic humor or mental runaway, and we have either a hero's illusion thwarted by a superior reality or a clash of two illusions." But *The Playboy* ends with something of Frye's third phase, too, as the *senex iratus* "gives way to the young man's desires." We can't see everything from the abstractive "middle distance," but Frye's typology makes a fine dictionary for this level of *The Playboy*'s style.

Synge grounded or rediscovered those conventions in an intensely local naturalism. His earlier plays had achieved somewhat similar syntheses—in the symbolic economy of *Riders to the Sea,* in the anecdotal spareness of the comedies. Lady Gregory's Kiltartan versions of Molière also provided partial examples—as did her farces of Irish gossip, *Spreading the News* (which she first thought would be a tragedy) and *Hyacinth Halvey*. Synge's own complex interest in what he called "the psychic state of the locality" did the rest. As a performance of *The Playboy* begins, the naturalism of setting, situation, and vocabulary seems to be dominant—and we never lose the sense of that inclusive frame. But our expectations are swiftly expanded by an alert speech that can flicker into farce, lyricism, satire, or pathos, by a rich and self-conscious fantasy that all characters share in varying degrees, by the constantly shifting perspectives that involve us (as J. L. Styan demonstrates) in the total action, and by the larger orchestration of moods or "currents" to which Synge devoted much attention in his preliminary notes. The play has fused the particular and the archetypal, naturalistic intimacy and comic distance. Hence its strange use of violence, which requires us to experience the painful meaning of our accepted conventions of farce; hence its poignantly comic reversals, abandonments, and reconciliations; hence its dynamic and interior exploration of a naively perceptive *miles gloriosus*. The growth and self-transcendence of Christy, which needs an effective stage-time much more rapid than naturalistic clock-time, is itself a function of the play's own expansion of mode. The resulting tonal ambivalence, as Synge knew, may recall *The Merchant of Venice* or *The Misanthrope;* but it is reached through a stylistic ambivalence quite unlike anything in Shakespeare or Molière. The play demands that a production find an appropriately balanced style of playing—one that remains in touch with the naturalistic ground but also moves toward the gracefully distanced choreography of farce.

"The aim of literature," Synge once said, "is to make the impossible seem inevitable or to make the inevitable seem impossible." Because *The Playboy*'s grotesque style contains a good bit of both, we are continually tempted to simplify it in one direction or another. Padraic Colum felt that the somewhat "sardonic" Christy of W. G. Fay (the actor whom Synge had in mind for the part, and who received the benefit of Synge's advice) detracted from "the extravagance of the comedy" and that the "horribly-bloodied bandage" on Old Mahon's head "took the whole thing out of the atmosphere of high comedy." He preferred the Abbey production of 1909, when Old Mahon "was made a less bloody object" and Fred O'Donovan's Christy had more innocent "charm and gaiety." And Colum's feeling was shared by such different judges as Joseph Holloway and George Moore. O'Donovan, said Moore, "was no doubt occasionally against the words, but that was unavoidable; the part cannot be played any other way." Moore himself even presumed to ask Maire O'Neill (Molly Allgood, who had played Pegeen from the beginning) to mitigate in 1909 the reversals of Act III: "I wonder if you could speak your words so that the audience would understand that your anger against Christy was simulated?" She didn't think she could. But later Abbey performances, if one may judge from P. P. Howe's comment in 1912, further reduced the play's complexity through cuts and the overplaying of comic business.

In 1939 the critic for the *New Statesman and Nation* found Ashley Dukes' London production too "naturalistic," insufficiently "flamboyant." But unlike Colum or Moore, he was not asking for a less painful tone. Cusack's Christy, he said, "was wilful, but excellent . . . at once rueful and swaggering"—though with "less violence than volatility." But he regretted that Pegeen, who "should have a touch of the fury in her," was played by Pamela Gibson "as a limpid young girl." In contrast the Widow Quin (a role now assumed by Maire O'Neill, after many years as Pegeen) had "a gloomy richness that overtowered Miss Gibson temperamentally." We can add today, of course, that Siobhán McKenna (in Cusack's production of 1954, and at the Dublin Theatre Festival of 1960 with Donal Donelly) has since returned to Pegeen's role a necessary vibrant depth and wildness.

The many-sidedness of the grotesque style, in fact, provided a strange challenge to Synge himself in 1905 and 1906. How should a play of such protean sympathies end? Synge's notes (which Ann Saddlemyer has assembled) read like the combinations and permutations in Frye's *Anatomy*: "Pegeen hesitates between Christy and Shawn. Marries Shawn, marries Old Man, or goes out with Christy." Or again: "Pegeen scoffs Christy and the Widow Quin takes him into her care." Then he tried expanding the plot to include a proposal by Widow Quin to Michael James, with the widow seemingly to become Christy's mother-in-law, and a final reversal in which "old Michael James renounces Widow Quin so she takes Christy instead." Only by late spring of 1906 did he pose these possibilities: Christy is "dragged away to . . . justice," or "set free by Widow Quin Old Mahon being really dead," or "Old Mahon revives on stage and there is grotesque scene of the two of them on their knees"—whereupon "They shake hands on a prodigiously fantastic treaty of amity and curtain on that." [1]

Synge's final shaping of Christy's end—"Ten thousand blessings upon all that's here, for you've turned me a likely gaffer in the end of all, the way I'll go romancing through a romping lifetime from this hour to the dawning of the judgment day"—does not ask to be taken simply as the resolution of a naturalistic story. Both Christy and the play have expanded beyond that perspective—though it remains to suggest irony and pathos beneath the exuberance. Nor does that end simply endorse a myth of the self-constructed man or the hero at dialectical odds with society: the play itself does not so easily abandon the grotesque world of the stage. And yet the final Christy is no baseless fantasy: his growth within the terms provided by that world has a strange cogency. His movement through role-playing to the ambiguous authenticity of romance becomes an image, I think, of our own participation in the richer movement of the entire dramatic event.

The Playboy's "action," its quasi-Stanislavskian "objective," might be called the desire "to play the comedy to the end of all." That peculiarly self-conscious and histrionic action is shared by each character in shifting ways. Each wants to discover in himself a comic or romantic role, to witness his own "play"—of which the self-delighting and expansive speech is a pervasive sign. (Christy with his glass is here a dominant image.) But each character is also a fascinated witness of the "play" of others, encouraging or provoking it by various means. And as Pegeen says with more inclusive truth than she intends, "It's queer joys they have, and who knows the thing they'd do . . ." The gamut of comic play runs from killing to wedding—from the romantic murder and sadistic farce in which an anxiously repressive and frustrated

[1] From *Collected Works: Plays,* edited by Ann Saddlemyer (London, 1968), pp. 298, 299, 301, 303–4. Copyright Oxford University Press 1968. Reprinted by permission of Oxford University Press.

society finds release, through subtler kinds of "playing upon" others (to tease, entrap, explore, or woo), to the more genuine "playing with" that arises from the mutual discovery of loneliness and reciprocal identity: "We're alike, so."

Each note in that scale reverberates in our own responses to the play—including what Synge once called "the thin relish of delightful sympathy with the wildness of evil which all feel but few acknowledge even to themselves." If much of our comic play comes from *The Playboy*'s allowing us to transcend the limited perspective of each character, *The Playboy* also treats *us* as it treats its characters—turning the tables upon us, undercutting our delight, showing us our vain and grotesque face in its glass. And behind all that playful counterpoint moves the desire for finality that flowers in the hyperbolic metaphors, in such phrases as "the end of all," "the end of time," and "the dawning of the judgment day," and in the heightened style of the stage action itself. Through the dissonance of the grotesque, we strive toward the ultimate harmony of romance.

Contrapuntal to Christy's version of that shared action is Pegeen's. His growth through the discovery of role-playing is balanced by her vigorously sustained but ambivalent play as she half-creates, holds, and then loses her man. Her opening speech toys imaginatively with the end of her self-defined romance—but we soon see that she lacks a real partner. Her second kind of play—the scornful teasing of Shawn, echoed in her acquiescent witnessing of his farcical entrapment—arises from her own frustration. Those two kinds of play then interact, expand, and lead toward a third. She pries the secret from the strangely Shawn-like Christy, identifies his shy violence with her dream of desire's release, engineers his employment, and ejects Shawn. Then she grows toward the fresh play of mutuality in the first of those lyric climaxes which are also major stages in Christy's growth, but turns swiftly and cagily to defend her new property against Widow Quin. In Act II, yet more on the defensive, she ejects her rivals and uses her skill in role-playing to intimidate and recapture her pot-boy hero—only to be diverted (after the second lyric climax, another stage in their reciprocal growth) by the stratagem of Shawn and Widow Quin.

The final sardonic and poignant amplification of such mixed play occurs in Act III. In the third lyric climax, Pegeen fully discovers the heart's wonder in her own histrionic glass. That moment is her fullest equivalent of Christy's more complex growth through role-playing. But she soon turns on him—in embarrassment and disappointment over his lie, in harder condemnation and self-justification over his second "murder." Rejecting the "dirty deed" that he thought would redeem himself in her eyes, she vents upon him all the violence of frustration that his "gallous story" had vicariously expressed for her—and more. When she forces herself to burn his leg, that action (more violent than any off-stage "murder") is crucial for them and for us. Our lust for farce and romantic cruelty—which has been mirrored verbally in such things as Marcus Quin's "maiming ewes," Jimmy Farrell's hanging his dog, Pegeen's description of Christy's hanging, and Sarah Tansey's driving ten miles to see "the man bit the yellow lady's nostril"—now shows its full face.

Partly through that burning, and through reconciliation with Old Mahon, Christy becomes fully the "playboy" and vanishes from the stage society—not into the "desert" of Molière's Alceste or the "night" of Shaw's Marchbanks, but into the realm of companionable romance. Pegeen, however, playing out her comedy of frustrated romanticism to its appropriate end, condemns herself to isolation within that society. Her startling blow and her wild lament are the play's final gestures. *The Playboy* in its sanity has not merely followed the "playboy." It has invited us to discover in ourselves, with increasing sympathy, irony, and painful gaiety, these two mutually dependent roles. That discovery is part of our own grotesque reconciliation—"We're alike, so"—as we play our comedy to the end of all.

But our reconciliation includes more. Widow Quin is for Pegeen a "sneaky kind" of murderer and man-stealer; and at first she may seem to us little more than a Mayo version of that stagey type. But in this play the static types are strangely dynamic: every seeming opposite is a secret double—and may prove to be an ally. Though Widow Quin's mode of playing is a tougher version of Pegeen's, it is really not more grasping or less open to new insights. Before Pegeen turns against Christy, the older temptress has begun to seem his double and his maternal savior. By the end of Act II she has sent away Old Mahon as well as Pegeen, and she has bargained with Christy as well as with Shawn. Her closing soliloquy (which counterpoints Christy's at the end of Act I—"it's great luck and company I've won me in the end of time") shares with us her present readiness to play out a new comedy: "Well, if the worst comes in the end of all, it'll be great game to see there's none to pity him but a widow woman, the like of me, has buried her children and destroyed her man." It is not merely ironic that Christy can say to this lonely woman as he said to Pegeen: "You're like me, so."

Thanks to Widow Quin's perspective, Act II also prepares us for the parallel reversal of that other negative type, Old Mahon. As she playfully draws him out (and we recall how Pegeen drew Christy out) the dialogue interweaves the differences and similarities between father and son. Her description of that son hiding behind the door—"A hideous, fearful villain, and the spit of you" —summarizes with affectionate humor for her and us their childlike self-inflation, naive folly, and real violence. In Act III Widow Quin takes Old Mahon a step further when she persuades him that he's a "sniggering maniac." His cheerfully proud acceptance of that fate ("there'll be a welcome before me, I tell you") foreshadows his final acceptance of the role of "heathen slave" to Christy's "gallant captain," in the reversal that expresses their new-found mutuality. "Is it me?" he will then ask (as he had asked when Widow Quin marvelled over his wickedness, and as Christy had asked when Pegeen praised his "noble brow"), and he will continue: "Glory be to God! (*With a broad smile.*) I am crazy again!" For him as for us, to role-play one's craziness is to journey toward sanity.

Amid such parallels and reversals, where every new discovery of identity is the discovery of a new reciprocity and a new role, we can't separate ourselves even from the lesser and more truly static characters. They often express our own momentary point of view; and their comic vanity, self-pity, or cruelty is never theirs alone. Perhaps the least sympathetic is Shawn, who thinks he wants a wedding that will end "trouble" (a version of Michael James' more affable desire for the peace of intoxication) but who really enjoys playing the role of anxious child, inviting the attention of parental surrogates and contemptuous baiters. But even Shawn has a whining lyricism ("and I'm after feeling a kind of fellow above in the furzy ditch"), and that fellow, the Christy who exits like a Mahon, entered much like Shawneen. Having lived through his own self-pity, longing for attention, baiting and being baited, Christy can include Shawn in his final "blessings." We can do no less, though we also share Pegeen's desire to give him a hard box on the ear.

As we respond to these role-playing characters, whose gestures are clarified and pointed by a language always alert to its own excesses, we discover ourselves in each fragment of Synge's histrionic glass. The "imitated" action of *The Playboy* portrays a society that the playboy himself must transcend, the father reconciled but the bride unredeemed. But in the performance of *The Playboy* a more inclusive society finds in itself the full gamut of the grotesque as it moves toward that openness which is equivalent to Christy's final state. When the curtain falls, we have seen that nothing human can be alien to us.

Perhaps Synge gives another turn to the process that C. L. Barber has elucidated in *Shakespeare's Festive Comedy*. As the playboy is to that Mayo community, so the play is to us; but the abortive saturnalia of that "imitated" action is completed by the action of performance. Our lord of misrule and potential scapegoat, *The Playboy* leads us through controlled and reflected release toward self-understanding. Has Synge, with a peculiarly modern self-consciousness, brought the conventions of saturnalian comedy back toward their presumed origins in the "psychic state" of the folk milieu? Whether or not he ever put it that way to himself, the notion doesn't seem beyond a writer who followed d'Arbois de Jubainville's lectures on mythology at the Sorbonne, and who could speculate on Dionysus while visiting Puck Fair. Presiding over the fair (as the essay "In West Kerry" tells us) was "Puck himself, a magnificent he-goat (Irish puc)" installed upon a platform. And there, "where the crowd was thickest, a young ballad-singer was howling a ballad in honour of Puck, making one think of the early Greek festivals, since the time of which, it is possible, the goat has been exalted yearly in Killorglin." Synge transcribed in full that ballad, which tells how "the lads and lassies coming gaily to Killorglin can be seen,/To view the Puck upon the stage, as our hero dressed in green."

In any case, our puckish Christy transcends that stage as he romps on toward the "dawning of the judgment day." And that image focuses the emergent end of Synge's orchestrated play. For *The Playboy* the ultimate harmony of romance and judgment is now, at the end of time within time, whenever we recognize our participation in the dissonances of the grotesque. On the play's own terms, such openness leads us past the manipulative forms of role-playing toward growth and mutuality. Yeats thought Synge to be one "in whom there is a perpetual 'Last Day,' a trumpeting, and coming up to judgment." The play invites us to share its grotesque version of that state.

Such, I suspect, is the implicit *telos* of this kind of playing, its journey and its journey's end. Playing with *The Playboy* we discover intentions that we didn't know we had. "Well, the heart's a wonder," says Pegeen. And at the height of his romance with her, Christy Mahon understandably feels "a kind of pity for the Lord God is all ages sitting lonesome in his golden chair." But Christy's theology has dropped from view the divine consort, that creative Wisdom who said: "I was by his side, a master craftsman, delighting him day after day, ever at play in his presence . . ." It is possible that *The Playboy of the Western World* (written by a skeptic, but one who hoped to translate an essay on role-playing called *De Imitatione Christi*) participates more than Christy knows in that immanent Wisdom "at play everywhere in his world, delighting to be with the sons of men."

PART ONE

From Ireland to the World

J. M. Synge and the Ireland of His Time

by William Butler Yeats

I

On Saturday, January 26, 1907, I was lecturing in Aberdeen, and when my lecture was over I was given a telegram which said, "Play great success." It had been sent from Dublin after the second act of *The Playboy of the Western World,* then being performed for the first time. After one in the morning, my host brought to my bedroom this second telegram, "Audience broke up in disorder at the word shift." I knew no more until I got the Dublin papers on my way from Belfast to Dublin on Tuesday morning. On the Monday night no word of the play had been heard. About forty young men had sat in the front seats of the pit, and stamped and shouted and blown trumpets from the rise to the fall of the curtain. On the Tuesday night also the forty young men were there. They wished to silence what they considered a slander upon Ireland's womanhood. Irish women would never sleep under the same roof with a young man without a chaperon, nor admire a murderer, nor use a word like "shift"; nor could any one recognise the country men and women of Davis and Kickham in these poetical, violent, grotesque persons, who used the name of God so freely, and spoke of all things that hit their fancy.

A patriotic journalism which had seen in Synge's capricious

"J. M. Synge and the Ireland of his Time" by William Butler Yeats. From Essays and Introductions *(New York: The Macmillan Company, 1961), pp. 311–14, 318–23, 326–28, 333–40.*

imagination the enemy of all it would have young men believe, had for years prepared for this hour, by that which is at once the greatest and most ignoble power of journalism, the art of repeating a name again and again with some ridiculous or evil association. The preparation had begun after the first performance of *The Shadow of the Glen,* Synge's first play, with an assertion made in ignorance, but repeated in dishonesty, that he had taken his fable and his characters, not from his own mind nor that profound knowledge of cot and curragh he was admitted to possess, but "from a writer of the Roman decadence." Some spontaneous dislike had been but natural, for genius like his can but slowly, amid what it has of harsh and strange, set forth the nobility of its beauty, and the depth of its compassion; but the frenzy that would have silenced his master-work was, like most violent things, artificial, that defence of virtue by those who have but little, which is the pomp and gallantry of journalism and its right to govern the world.

As I stood there watching, knowing well that I saw the dissolution of a school of patriotism that held sway over my youth, Synge came and stood beside me, and said, "A young doctor has just told me that he can hardly keep himself from jumping on to a seat, and pointing out in that howling mob those whom he is treating for venereal disease."

II

Thomas Davis, whose life had the moral simplicity which can give to actions the lasting influence that style alone can give to words, had understood that a country which has no national institutions must show its young men images for the affections, although they be but diagrams of what should be or may be. He and his school imagined the Soldier, the Orator, the Patriot, the Poet, the Chieftain, and above all the Peasant; and these, as celebrated in essays and songs and stories, possessed so many virtues that no matter how England, who, as Mitchel said, "had the ear of the world," might slander us, Ireland, even though she could not come at the world's other ear, might go her way unabashed. But ideas and images which have to be understood and loved by large numbers of people must appeal to no rich personal experience, no patience of study, no delicacy of sense; and if at rare moments some *Memory of the Dead* can take its strength from one, at all other moments manner and matter will be rhetorical, conventional, sentimental; and language, because it is carried beyond life perpetually, will be worn and cold like the thought, with unmeaning pedantries and silences, and a dread of all that has salt and savour. After a while, in a land that has given itself to agitation overmuch, abstract thoughts are raised up between men's minds and Nature, who never does the same thing twice, or makes one man like another, till minds, whose patriotism is perhaps great enough to carry them to the scaffold, cry down natural impulse with the morbid persistence of minds unsettled by some fixed idea. They are preoccupied with the nation's future, with heroes, poets, soldiers, painters, armies, fleets, but only as these things are understood by a child in a National School, while a secret feeling that what is so unreal needs continual defence makes them bitter and restless. They are like some State which has only paper money, and seeks by punishments to make it buy whatever gold can buy. They no longer love, for only life is loved, and at last a generation is like an hysterical woman who will make unmeasured accusations and believe impossible things, because of some logical deduction from a solitary thought which has turned a portion of her mind to stone. . . .

IV

I attack things that are as dear to many as some holy image carried hither and thither by some broken clan, and can but say that I have felt in my body the affections I disturb, and believed that if I could raise them into contemplation I would make possible a literature that, finding its subject-matter all ready in men's minds, would be, not as ours is, an interest for scholars, but the possession of a people. I have founded societies with this aim, and was indeed founding one in Paris when I first met with J. M. Synge, and I have known what it is to be changed by that I would have changed, till I became argumentative and unmannerly, hating men even in daily life for their opinions. And though I was never convinced that the anatomies of last year's leaves are a living forest, nor thought a continual apologetic could do other than make the soul a vapour and the body a stone, nor believed that literature can be made by anything but by what is still blind and dumb within ourselves, I have had to learn how hard, in one who lives where forms of expression and habits of thought have been born, not for the pleasure of begetting, but for the public good, is that purification from insincerity, vanity, malignity, arrogance, which is the discovery of style. But life became sweet again when I had learnt all I had not learnt in shaping words, in defending Synge against his enemies, and knew that rich energies, fine, turbulent or gracious thoughts, whether in life or letters, are but love-children.

Synge seemed by nature unfitted to think a political thought, and with the exception of one sentence, spoken when I first met him in Paris, that implied some sort of Nationalist conviction, I cannot remember that he spoke of politics or showed any interest in men in the mass, or an any subject that is studied through abstractions and statistics. Often for months together he and I and Lady Gregory would see no one outside the Abbey Theatre, and that life, lived as it were in a ship at sea, suited him, for unlike those whose habit of mind fits them to judge of men in the mass, he was wise in judging individual men, and as wise in dealing with them as the faint energies of ill-health would permit; but of their political thoughts he long understood nothing. One night, when we were still producing plays in a little hall, certain members of the company told him that a play on the Rebellion of '98 would be a great success. After a fortnight he brought them a scenario which read like a chapter out of Rabelais. Two women, a Protestant and a Catholic, take refuge in a cave, and there quarrel about religion, abusing the Pope or Queen Elizabeth and Henry VIII, but in low voices, for the one fears to be ravished by the soldiers, the other by the rebels. At last one woman goes out because she would sooner any fate than such wicked company. Yet I doubt if he would have written at all if he did not write of Ireland, and for it, and I know that he thought creative art could only come from such preoccupation. Once when, in later years, anxious about the educational effect of our movement, I proposed adding to the Abbey Company a second company to play international drama, Synge, who had not hitherto opposed me, thought the matter so important that he did so in a formal letter.

I had spoken of a German municipal theatre as my model, and he said that the municipal theatres all over Europe gave fine performances of old classics, but did not create (he disliked modern drama for its sterility of speech, and perhaps ignored it), and that we would create nothing if we did not give all our thoughts to Ireland. Yet in Ireland he loved only what was wild in its people, and in "the grey and wintry sides of many glens." All the rest, all that one reasoned over, fought for, read of in leading articles, all that came from education, all that came down from Young Ireland—though for this he had not lacked a little sympathy—first wakened in him perhaps that irony which runs through all he wrote; but once awakened, he made it turn its face upon the whole of life. The women quarrelling in the cave would not have amused him if something in his nature had not looked out on most disputes, even those wherein he himself took sides, with a mischievous wisdom. He told me once that when he lived in some peasant's house, he tried to make those about him forget that he was there, and it is certain that he was silent in any crowded room. It is possible that low vitality helped him to be observant and contemplative, and made him dislike, even in solitude, those thoughts which unite us to others, much as we all dislike, when fatigue or illness has sharpened the nerves, hoardings covered with advertisements, the fronts of big theatres, big London hotels, and all architecture which has been made to impress the crowd. What blindness did for Homer, lameness for Hephaestus, asceticism for any saint you will, bad health did for him by making him ask no more of life than that it should keep him living, and above all perhaps by concentrating his imagination upon one thought, health itself. I think that all noble things are the result of warfare; great nations and classes, of warfare in the visible world, great poetry and philosophy, of invisible warfare, the division of a mind within itself, a victory, the sacrifice of a man to himself. I am certain that my friend's noble art, so full of passion and heroic beauty, is the victory of a man who in poverty and sickness created from the delight of expression, and in the contemplation that is born of the minute and delicate arrangement of images, happiness and health of mind. Some early poems have a morbid melancholy, and he himself spoke of early work he had destroyed as morbid, for as yet the craftsmanship was not fine enough to bring the artist's joy which is of one substance with that of sanctity. In one poem he waits at some street-corner for a friend, a woman perhaps, and while he waits and gradually understands that nobody is coming, he sees two funerals and shivers at the future; and in another, written on his twenty-fifth birthday, he wonders if the twenty-five years to come shall be as evil as those gone by. Later on, he can see himself as but a part of the spectacle of the world and mix into all he sees that flavour of extravagance, or of humour, or of philosophy, that makes one understand that he contemplates even his own death as if it were another's and finds in his own destiny but, as it were, a projection through a burning-glass of that general to men. There is in the creative joy an acceptance of what life brings, because we have understood the beauty of what it brings, or a hatred of death for what it takes away, which arouses within us, through some sympathy perhaps with all other men, an energy so noble, so powerful, that we laugh aloud and mock, in the terror or the sweetness of our exaltation, at death and oblivion.

In no modern writer that has written of Irish life before him, except, it may be, Miss Edgeworth in *Castle Rackrent,* was there anything to change a man's thought about the world or stir his moral nature, for they but play with pictures, persons and events, that whether well or ill observed are but an amusement for the mind where it escapes from meditation, a child's show that makes the fables of his art as significant by contrast as some procession painted on an Egyptian wall; for in these fables, an intelligence on which the tragedy of the world had been thrust in so few years that Life had no time to brew her sleepy drug has spoken of the moods that are the expression of its wisdom. All minds that have a wisdom come of tragic reality seem morbid to those that are accustomed to writers who have not faced reality at all; just as the saints, with that Obscure Night of the Soul, which fell so certainly that they numbered it among spiritual states, one among other ascending steps, seem morbid to the rationalist and the old-fashioned Protestant controversialist. The thoughts of journalists, like the thoughts of the Irish novelists, are neither healthy nor unhealthy, not having risen to that state where either is possible, nor should we call them happy; for who, if happiness were not the supreme attainment of man, would have sought it in heroic toils, in the cell of the ascetic, or imagined it above the cheerful newspapers, above the clouds? . . .

IX

As I read *The Aran Islands* right through for the first time since he showed it me in manuscript, I come to understand how much knowledge of the real life of Ireland went to the creation of a world which is yet as fantastic as the Spain of Cervantes. Here is the story of *The Playboy,* of *The Shadow of the Glen*; here is the ghost on horseback and the finding of the young man's body of *Riders to the Sea,* numberless ways of speech and vehement pictures that had seemed to owe nothing to observation, and all to some overflowing of himself, or to some mere necessity of dramatic construction. I had thought the violent quarrels of *The Well of the Saints* came from his love of bitter condiments, but here is a couple that quarrel all day long amid neighbours who gather as for a play. I had defended the burning of Christy Mahon's leg on the ground that an artist need but make his characters self-consistent, and yet that too was observation, for "although these people are kindly towards each other and their children, they have no sympathy for the suffering of animals, and little sympathy for pain when the person who feels it is not in danger." I had thought it was in the wantonness of fancy Martin Doul accused the smith of plucking his living ducks, but a few lines farther on, in this book where moral indignation is unknown, I read, "Sometimes when I go into a cottage, I find all the women of the place down on their knees plucking the feathers from live ducks and geese."

He loves all that has edge, all that is salt in the mouth, all that is rough to the hand, all that heightens the emotions by contest, all that stings into life the sense of tragedy; and in this book, unlike the plays where nearness to his audience moves him to mischief, he shows it without thought of other taste than his. It is so constant, it is all set out so simply, so naturally, that it suggests a correspondence between a lasting mood of the soul and this life that shares the harshness of rocks and wind. The food of the spiritual-minded is sweet, an Indian scripture says, but passionate minds love bitter food. Yet he is no indifferent observer, but is certainly kind and sympathetic to all about him. When an old and ailing man, dreading the coming winter, cries at his leaving, not thinking to see him again, and he notices that the old man's mitten has a hole in it where the palm is accustomed to the stick, one knows that it is with eyes full of interested affection as befits a simple man and not in the curiosity of study. When he had left the Blaskets for the last time, he travelled with a lame pensioner who had drifted there, why Heaven knows, and one morning having missed him from the inn where they were staying, he believed he had gone back to the island, and searched everywhere and questioned everybody, till he understood of a sudden that he was jealous as though the island were a woman.

The book seems dull if you read much at a time, as the later Kerry essays do not, but nothing that he has written recalls so completely to my senses the man as he was in daily life; and as I read, there are moments when every line of his face, every inflection of his voice, grows so clear in memory that I cannot realise that he is dead. He was no nearer when we walked and talked than now while I read these unarranged, unspeculating pages, wherein the only life he loved with his whole heart reflects itself as in the still water of a pool. Thought comes to him slowly, and only after long seemingly unmeditative watching, and when it comes (and he had the same character in matters of business), it is spoken without hesitation and never changed. His conversation was not an experimental thing, an instrument of research, and this made him silent; while his essays recall events, on which one feels that he pronounces no judgment even in the depth of his own mind, because the labour of Life itself had not yet brought the philosophic generalisation which was almost as much his object as the emotional generalisation of beauty. A mind that generalises rapidly, continually prevents the experience that would have made it feel and see deeply, just as a man whose character is too complete in youth seldom grows into any energy of moral beauty. Synge had indeed no obvious ideals, as these are understood by young men, and even, as I think, disliked them, for he once complained to me that our modern poetry was but the poetry "of the lyrical boy," and this lack makes his art have a strange wildness and coldness, as of a man born in some far-off spacious land and time. . . .

XII

In all drama which would give direct expression to reverie, to the speech of the soul with itself, there is some device that checks the rapidity of dialogue. When Oedipus speaks out of the most vehement passions, he is conscious of the presence of the Chorus, men before whom he must keep up appearances, "children latest born of Cadmus' line" who do not share his passion. Nobody is hurried or breathless. We listen to reports and discuss them, taking part as it were in a council of State. Nothing happens before our eyes. The dignity of Greek drama, and in a lesser degree of that of Corneille and Racine, depends, as contrasted with the troubled life of Shakespearian drama, on an almost even speed of dialogue, and on a so continuous exclusion of the animation of common life that thought remains lofty and language rich. Shakespeare, upon whose stage everything may happen, even the blinding of Gloucester, and who has no formal check except what is implied in the slow, elaborate structure of blank verse, obtains time for reverie by an often encumbering euphuism, and by such a loosening of his plot as will give his characters the leisure to look at life from without. Maeterlinck—to name the first modern of the old way who comes to mind—reaches the same end, by choosing instead of human beings persons who are as faint as a breath upon a looking-glass, symbols who can speak a language slow and heavy with dreams because their own life is but a dream. Modern drama, on the other hand, which accepts the tightness of the classic plot, while expressing life directly, has been driven to make indirect its expression of the mind, which it leaves to be inferred from some commonplace sentence or gesture as we infer it in ordinary life; and this is, I believe, the cause of the perpetual disappointment of the hope imagined this hundred years that France or Spain or Germany or Scandinavia would at last produce the master we await.

The divisions in the arts are almost all in the first instance technical, and the great schools of drama have been divided from one another by the form or the metal of their mirror, by the check chosen for the rapidity of dialogue. Synge found the check that suited his temperament in an elaboration of the dialects of Kerry and Aran. The cadence is long and meditative, as befits the thought of men who are much alone, and who when they meet in one another's houses—as their way is at the day's end—listen patiently, each man speaking in turn and for some little time, and taking pleasure in the vaguer meaning of the words and in their sound. Their thought, when not merely practical, is as full of traditional wisdom and extravagant pictures as that of some Aeschylean chorus, and no matter what the topic is, it is as though the present were held at arm's length. It is the reverse of rhetoric, for the speaker serves his own delight, though doubtless he would tell you that like Raftery's whiskey-drinking it was but for the company's sake. A medicinal manner of speech, too, for it could not even express, so little abstract it is and so rammed with life, those worn generalisations of National propaganda.

> I'll be telling you the finest story you'd hear any place from Dundalk to Ballinacree with great queens in it, making themselves matches from the start to the end, and they with shiny silks on them. . . . I've a grand story of the great queens of Ireland, with white necks on them the like of Sarah Casey, and fine arms would hit you a slap. . . . What good am I this night, God help me? What good are the grand stories I have when it's few would listen to an old woman, few but a girl maybe would be in great fear the time her hour was come, or little child wouldn't be sleeping with the hunger on a cold night?

That has the flavour of Homer, of the Bible, of Villon, while Cervantes would have thought it sweet in the mouth though not his food. This use of Irish dialect for noble purpose by Synge, and by Lady Gregory, who had it already in her *Cuchulain of Muirthemne,* and by Dr. Hyde in those first translations he has not equalled since, has done much for national dignity. When I was a boy I was often troubled and sorrowful because Scottish dialect was capable of noble use, but the Irish of obvious roystering humour only; and this error fixed on my imagination by so many novelists and rhymers made me listen badly. Synge wrote down words and phrases wherever he went, and with that knowledge of Irish which made all our country idioms easy to his hand, found it so rich a thing that he had begun translating into it fragments of the great literatures of the world, and had planned a complete version of *The Imitation of Christ*. It gave him imaginative richness and yet left to him the sting and tang of reality. How vivid in his translation from Villon are those "eyes with a big gay look out of them would bring folly from a great scholar"! More vivid surely than anything in Swinburne's version, and how noble those words which are yet simple country speech, in which his Petrarch mourns that death came upon Laura just as time was making chastity easy, and the day come when "lovers may sit together and say out all things are in their hearts," and "my sweet enemy was making a start, little by little, to give over her great wariness, the way she was wringing a sweet thing out of my sharp sorrow."

XIII

I remember saying once to Synge that though it seemed to me that a conventional descriptive passage encumbered the action at the moment of crisis, I liked *The Shadow of the Glen* better than *Riders to the Sea,* that seemed for all the nobility of its end, its mood of Greek tragedy, too passive in suffering, and had quoted from Matthew Arnold's introduction to *Empedocles on Etna* to prove my point. Synge answered: "It is a curious thing that *Riders to the Sea* succeeds with an English but not with an Irish audience, and *The Shadow of the Glen,* which is not liked by an English audience, is always liked in Ireland, though it is disliked there in theory." Since then *Riders to the Sea* has grown into great popularity in Dublin, partly because, with the tactical instinct of an Irish mob, the demonstrators against *The Playboy* both in the Press and in the theatre, where it began the evening, selected it for applause. It is now what Shelley's *Cloud* was for many years, a comfort to those who do not like to deny altogether the genius they cannot understand. Yet I am certain that, in the long run, his grotesque plays with their lyric beauty, their violent laughter, *The Playboy of the Western World* most of all, will be loved for holding so much of the mind of Ireland. Synge has written of *The Playboy*: "Any one who has lived in real intimacy with the Irish peasantry will know that the wildest sayings in this play are tame indeed compared with the fancies one may hear at any little hillside cottage of Geesala, or Carraroe, or Dingle Bay." It is the strangest, the most beautiful expression in drama of that Irish fantasy which overflowing through all Irish literature that has come out of Ireland itself (compare the fantastic Irish account of the Battle of Clontarf with the sober Norse account) is the unbroken character of Irish genius. In modern days this genius has delighted in mischievous extravagance, like that of the Gaelic poet's curse upon his children: "There are three things that I hate: the Devil that is waiting for my soul; the worms that are waiting for my body; my children, who are waiting for my wealth and care neither for my body nor my soul: O, Christ, hang all in the same noose!" I think those words were spoken with a delight in their vehemence that took out of anger half the bitterness with all the gloom. An old man on the Aran Islands told me the very tale on which *The Playboy* is founded, beginning with the words: "If any gentleman has done a crime we'll hide him. There was a gentleman that killed his father, and I had him in my own house six months till he got away to America." Despite the solemnity of his slow speech his eyes shone as the eyes must have shone in that Trinity College branch of the Gaelic League which began every meeting with prayers for the death of an old Fellow of College who disliked their movement, or as they certainly do when patriots are telling how short a time the prayers took to the killing of him. I have seen a crowd, when certain Dublin papers had wrought themselves into an imaginary loyalty, so possessed by what seemed the very genius of satiric fantasy that one all but looked to find some feathered heel among the cobble-stones. Part of the delight of crowd or individual is always that somebody will be angry, somebody take the sport for gloomy earnest. We are mocking at his solemnity, let us therefore so hide our malice that he may be more solemn still, and the laugh run higher yet. Why should we speak his language and so wake him from a dream of all those emotions which men feel because they should, and not because they must? Our minds, being sufficient to themselves, do not wish for victory but are content to elaborate our extravagance, if fortune aid, into wit or lyric beauty, and as for the rest, "There are nights when a king like Conchobar would spit upon his arm-ring and queens will stick out their tongues at the rising moon." This habit of the mind has made Oscar Wilde and Mr. Bernard Shaw the most celebrated makers of comedy to our time, and if it has sounded plainer still in the conversation of the one, and in some few speeches of the other, that is but because they have not been able to turn out of their plays an alien trick of zeal picked up in struggling youth. Yet, in Synge's plays also, fantasy gives the form and not the thought, for the core is always, as in all great art, an overpowering vision of certain virtues, and our capacity for sharing in that vision is the measure of our delight. Great art chills us at first by its coldness or its strangeness, by what seems capricious, and yet it is from these qualities it has authority, as though it had fed on locusts and wild honey. The imaginative writer shows us the world as a painter does his picture, reversed in a looking-glass, that we may see it, not as it seems to eyes habit has made dull, but as we were Adam and this the first morning; and when the new image becomes as little strange as the old we shall stay with him, because he has, besides the strangeness, not strange to him, that made us share his vision, sincerity that makes us share his feeling.

To speak of one's emotions without fear or moral ambition, to come out from under the shadow of other men's minds, to forget their needs, to be utterly oneself, that is all the Muses care for. Villon, pander, thief and man-slayer, is as immortal in their eyes, and illustrates in the cry of his ruin as great a truth, as Dante in abstract ecstasy, and touches our compassion more. All art is the disengaging of a soul from place and history, its suspension in a beautiful or terrible light to await the Judgment, though it must be, seeing that all its days were a Last Day, judged already. It may show the crimes of Italy as Dante did, or Greek mythology like Keats, or Kerry and Galway villages, and so vividly that ever after

I shall look at all with like eyes, and yet I know that Cino da Pistoia thought Dante unjust, that Keats knew no Greek, that those country men and women are neither so lovable nor so lawless as "mine author sung it me"; that I have added to my being, not my knowledge. . . .

Synge's Poetic Drama

by Una Ellis-Fermor

> . . . he had come
> Towards nightfall upon certain set apart
> In a most desolate stony place,
> Towards nightfall upon a race
> Passionate and simple like his heart.
>
> W. B. Yeats. (Lines on Synge in *Major Robert Gregory*.)

Synge is the only great poetic dramatist of the movement; the only one, that is, for whom poetry and drama were inseparable, in whose work dramatic intensity invariably finds poetic expression and the poetic mood its only full expression in dramatic form. All the other playwrights of the movement seem, in the last analysis, to have been either dramatists in whom the instinct for dramatic expression sometimes brought with it the poetry of diction, imagery, or cadence, or poets who turned for a time to the dramatic form, returning, sooner or later, again to other forms. But it is hard to imagine this separation in Synge; poetic and dramatic expression in him are one and simultaneous, as they appear to have been with Shakespeare and with Webster, in whom the presence of a high degree of one mood meant the presence of a high degree of the other, whether the form were prose or verse, the matter comedy or tragedy.

Yet there is a paradox in Synge's genius, a dualism of a different

---

"Synge's Poetic Drama" (original title: "John Millington Synge") by Una Ellis-Fermor. From The Irish Dramatic Movement, *2nd ed. (London: Methuen & Company, Ltd., 1954), pp. 163–79, in abridged form. First published, November, 1939. Second edition, 1954. Reprinted by permission of Associated Book Publishers Ltd.*

and a rarer kind. For while he is essentially a dramatic poet, one of the roots of his poetry is mysticism, such as he recognized in the mountain and sea-faring Irish peasants living far enough out of reach of civilization to respond to and reflect the nature about them. And mystical experience, particularly the extreme form of nature-mysticism that we find in Synge, is in itself as nearly as possible incompatible with dramatic expression. Yet the presence of nature is as strongly felt in the plays as in *The Aran Islands* and *In Wicklow and West Kerry* and it is not there as a digression, irrelevant or undramatic. Nature is a protagonist in *The Shadow of the Glen* and *Riders to the Sea,* so filling the minds of the characters as to shape their actions, moods and fates; it is the ever-present setting, genially familiar, of *The Well of the Saints* and *The Tinker's Wedding*; it remains as a continual and surprising source of imagery and incidental reference throughout *The Playboy* and becomes again a poetic protagonist in *Deirdre.* When Synge began to draw his material from the Aran Islands he had found, by one of those accidents of fortune which sometimes save genius from extinction, the people who alone could stimulate his imagination and offer him something on which this strange combination of dramatist and nature-mystic could work. They were the human theme which drama must have and yet they were in part at least nature itself.

Moreover, Synge, who thinks less than any of his predecessors about Nationalism[1] or the Gaelic League or the past civilizations of Ireland, is one of the few followers of the movement who, through affinity of spirit, seem to carry on unbroken the tradition of ancient Irish nature poetry. In that poetry a distinctive quality is the sense of intimacy between man and nature about him; animals, birds, trees, and flowers are not only a source of delight but almost a part of man himself.[2] And it is, paradoxically, in the descriptive imagery

[1] W. B. Yeats could only remember one remark of Synge's that could be interpreted as even partly political. (*Cutting of an Agate,* p. 142 and *Autobiographies,* p. 424.)

[2] The comparison with the early poetry of A.E. inevitably suggests itself at this point. The distinction I am trying to draw is between Synge's direct communion with physical nature and A.E.'s spiritualizing of natural forces, which begins as early as *Homeward, Songs by the Way,* and *The Earth Breath.* Synge's most explicit statement is perhaps that in the description of the seagulls in *The Aran Islands* (Vol. i, Allen and Unwin, 1921, p. 43).

of Synge, whose comedies are never wholly free from tragedy or tragic irony, that the happy, gay, and friendly relations with nature are to be found (as in the ancient poets) as clearly revealed as those fiercer or sterner moods which his contemporaries converted more often to pathetic or romantic poetic symbolism. For Synge, who perceives the intermittent savagery of human nature, and yet believes that, "Of all the things that nourish the imagination, humour is one of the most needful," finds little that is sad or wistful in the Celtic twilight. That twilight, against which Lady Gregory expostulated humorously in her turn, throws a curious mist over Irish scenery for those who view it from a distance. But Synge, who knew Ireland rather than what was written about Ireland, who understood profoundly the despondency and melancholy common in the Wicklow Hills,[3] reveals also, even in that earliest play, the brilliance and the strength of nature. For he, like the ancient poets his ancestors and like his own tinkers and beggars, the direct descendants of the ancient peasants, saw, as well as the mists of the Wicklow and the thunders of the sea upon the Aran Islands, a glad, bright, positive illumination. It is when we study his imagery that we recollect that *Maeve* is not the whole nor necessarily the truest picture of that ancient Ireland which, after all, contained also Saint Patrick, the king's brother who was a hermit and the monk who had a white cat. Synge does not dwell in the Celtic twilight because he belongs, not by sentiment and wistful longing, but by the roots of his nature to the Celtic noonday which had been sweet and sane. Any reader who goes back from the nature imagery of Synge to Kuno Meyer's translations of the old poetry, echoes again that great scholar's inspired comment, "the true history of Ireland has never yet been written"[4] and it then seems as though Martyn's backward gaze upon the ancient glories through a mist of regret not only sentimentalizes the hard genius of the race but dims the clear radiance that he would honour.

Synge stood alone, then, in this distinctive balance of nature-mystic and dramatic poet, a balance rare before him, though soon

[3] Descriptions and references to this run through *The Shadow of the Glen* and *In Wicklow and West Kerry*. Sometimes they are almost identical in substance and in phrasing in the play and in the prose writings.

[4] Introduction to *Ancient Irish Poetry,* p. xii.

after to be found in one or two English writers. It is, I think, something different from the combination, found from the Greeks to the Elizabethans, of dramatic poetry with an awareness and love of outdoor nature. Even when the love of nature is strong, as it is in poets as far apart otherwise as Aeschylus, Sophocles, Seneca, Shakespeare and many later dramatic poets, the sense of nature as a background, however close that background comes, is still distinct from the fusion that we find in Synge.[5] For in Synge natural beauty is not merely one of many forms of beauty that he loves or reveres, and nature is not merely a background in harmony with the play, a kind of setting kept before our eyes by allusions coming naturally out of the poet's own affection. It is an actor recognized by the other human actors, sometimes (as in the *Well of the Saints*) as a constant, familiar companion, sometimes (as in the *Shadow of the Glen* and *Riders to the Sea*) as a presence or even an agent who forms their moods or draws down their fates. Very few Irish cities are big enough, even now, to breed men ignorant of country life, and most Irishmen, to this day, are at heart countrymen, responsive to the familiar miracle of their own mountains, rivers, islands, and seas. But in Synge himself, as in A.E. and in the peasants with whom Synge was in natural sympathy, there is a reach of experience beyond this, and animals and birds, even the stranger powers of hills, mists, storms, and seas are accepted as part of the same creation as man himself, experiencing the same moods as he does and drawing him into their spirit. "In Inishmaan one is forced to believe in a sympathy between man and nature." He may consent or resist, but it is still himself.

There are many varieties of this relationship and nowhere does Synge show more clearly the extent of his own experience of nature than in the variety of portraits he gives of men's differing responses to what they all accept as a main part of their lives. There is an easy, comfortable friendliness in nature as it is known to the blind beggars of the *Well of the Saints*; it is their familiar companion and when, after having their sight for a while, they recover the blessed

[5] I can only call to mind one play, the *Oedipus Coloneus,* in which the function of nature is as intimate as in the plays of Synge; in the Elizabethans it appears to be, so far as I can judge, at most a significant setting, though often (as in *Lear*) in the closest harmony with the central idea of the play.

state of blindness, it is the warmth of the sun and the scent of the broom that gives them their greatest joy. . . .

The peasants of the Wicklow Hills look on nature with more awe. Those empty, misty mountains offer no easy relationship, but the people in *The Shadow of the Glen* never lose sight of that presence and betray a constant preoccupation with it, telling the time of day by the shadow moving up the glen and the sun sinking in the bog, and admitting as frankly their fear of the melancholy of the mountains that draws the imagination. No one is such a fool as to call that fancy in a country where men run mad and rush out in the mist to die alone in the mountains. And yet, even here, there are two different attitudes which reveal distinct experiences. Nora, who has lived in her cottage at the end of the glen, as in a garrison against the mountain's power, is terrified of the loneliness and the gloom; but the tramp who, like Wordsworth's shepherd, has been alone among the hearts of many hundred mists, has reached some kind of union, where, though there is still awe, there is also knowledge and love. Indeed the most interesting theme in the play is perhaps the study of her conversion from the terrified repudiation of nature by the power of the man who can at times at least identify himself with it. . . .

Nature in *Riders to the Sea* is yet more terrible to man, and it is beyond the power of any but the young men, who still have some of its own fierce hardness, to accept it. "It is the life of a young man to be going on the sea," and Bartley is filled with a hard fierce glory like that of the storm that devours him almost with his own consent. But the others are broken by it; Maurya's resignation is not that of love, hardly perhaps of understanding, but of relief that the end has come to a heroic contest, even if in defeat: "There isn't anything more the sea can do to me." In this play nature is the protagonist, the main actor and inevitably victorious. Yet it is not an alien thing responsible only for event, but something to which they have grown so akin that their familiarity with its ways takes all astonishment, all horror from their fate. It is the sea that is the real theme of the play and sometimes the human characters seem there only to reveal by their responses what its nature is, like a painting in which grass and trees and clouds serve by their colour and line to reveal the movement of the else invisible wind. . . .

In *The Playboy* the direct part played by nature is far less. It is by no means a main actor, hardly even an actor at all. Indeed, in such a play as this, a wild comedy, set, not in a lonely mountain-hut, but in a public house which is the social centre of its district, there would seem no place for the presence of nature. But Synge and his Mayo peasants know better than that, and their references, though sparser than those of a comedy of outdoor life like *The Well of the Saints,* are significant, perhaps because of their apparent detachment from the main subject. Men come in from the outdoor world into the lighted inn still mindful of the darkness and the silence broken by the breathing of sleeping cows, and they bring in that dark, enveloping outside world with them until we know that even there we are among people to whom being within doors is a temporary, almost an accidental, condition. We could draw the district around Flaherty's inn, simply from these constant, unobtrusive references, the shore and the wide shallow sands, the river and the stepping stones and the widow Quinn's cottage on the little hill, the only house within four miles by the road. They are delicate, natural, accurate observers and every man and woman in the play has familiar knowledge of nature's moods and habits. But it is Christy Mahon, the natural poet, who in this play has the fuller experience that belongs to Synge and to the peasants of the Aran Islands or of *Riders to the Sea.* For in his memory of the crisis of his life the picture of the place where it happened, the high windy corner of the distant hills, is more real for him and for us than the deed itself. He alters and expands the deed; it is subject to fantasy. But not the setting. The "cold, sloping, stony, divil's patch of a field" and the sun that "came out between the cloud and the hill and it shining green in my face," are not forgotten. This is a man for whom nature is not a background to life but an inseparable part of his keenest experience:

Pegeen. And it's that you'd call sport, is it, to be abroad in the darkness with yourself alone.

Christy. I'd be as happy as the sunshine of St. Martin's Day, watching the light passing in the north or the patches of fog, till I'd hear a rabbit starting to screech and I'd go running in the furze. Then, when I'd my full share, I'd come walking down where you'd see the ducks and geese stretched sleeping on the highway of the road.

Nature, no longer an actor in the play, has become an undertone, but one of a rather curious interest; for the brilliance of the colours, standing sharp and clear against each other and giving radiance each to each, convey, no less than the rich and glorious images and rhythms of the talk, the vitality and fertility which are the essence of the play. The "rich joy found only in what is superb and wild in reality" is revealed as much by the imagery as by the actions of the people.

In *Deirdre of the Sorrows* nature is as intimate a part of the people's life and speech as ever, but there is perhaps more definition, almost more consciousness in Synge's perception. For in the ancient Irish legends from which he drew for this play—and which he followed sometimes as faithfully as Shakespeare did the phrasing of Holinshed—he found an experience like his own. Just as his knowledge of the Aran Islanders helped him to understand the primitive yet aristocratic civilization of ancient Ulster, so his understanding of their relation to nature made him one, instantly, with the tradition of ancient Irish nature poetry; in this last play the nature experience of his life-time seems to meet and join hands with that undying tradition of Irish thought and poetry. It is no ornament. It is woven deep. And in the moments of intensest passion it seems more essential than the passion itself. . . .

Thus far, as has been suggested, the nature poetry of Synge's plays reveals experiences which, in their range and kind, are curiously like those of the ancient poetry of his own race. The allusions and descriptions in the comedies, a clear, gay, noonday poetry of nature, as sane as it is happy, can be matched in the poems translated by Kuno Meyer,[6] *King and Hermit, Summer has Come, Songs of Summer, Arran, The Blackbird, Columcille's Greeting to Ireland,*

[6] I have referred chiefly to the volume of translations *Ancient Irish Poetry,* published by Kuno Meyer in 1911, as being perhaps on the whole the most easily accessible to English readers. But all the translations of the Irish literature written between the eighth and the tenth centuries that I have read are full of such allusions and images, notably Dr. Hyde's two famous volumes and the recently published translations by Dr. Robin Flower (1931) and Mr. Frank O'Connor (1939).

The Scribe, and several others; the fiercer side, the glory and terror of storm and the violence of nature in such lines as the *Song of the Sea;* its remorseless bleakness in *A Song of Winter* or *Summer is Gone* and the familiar intimacy with nature, particularly that phase which sees animals and men as creatures separated by no barrier, sharing their experiences and sympathy, in *The Deserted Home* or *The Monk and his Pet Cat.* In the ancient poets, as in Synge, there is nothing sentimental or wistful; there is nothing to remind us of the Celtic twilight, probably because we are so often irradiated with the Celtic noonday. Perhaps in the ancient poetry there is less of the majesty and implacableness of nature by which man is so often accidentally destroyed, and more of that rare, robust quality of gladness. But the vividness of the experience, its depth and intimacy are the same in both:

> *Guare.* Why, hermit Marvan, sleepest thou not
> Upon a feather quilt?
> Why rather sleepest thou abroad,
> Upon a pitchpine floor?
>
> *Marvan.* I have a shieling in the wood
> None knows it save my God
> An ash-tree on the hither side, a hazel bush beyond,
> A huge old tree encompasses it.
>
> A choice pure spring and princely water
> To drink:
> There spring watercresses, yew-berries,
> Ivy bushes thick as a man.
>
> Fairest princes come to my house,
> A ready gathering:
> Pure water, perennial bushes,
> Salmon, trout.
>
> A bush of rowan, black sloes,
> Dusky blackthorns,
> Plenty of food, acorns, pure berries,
> Bare flags.
>
> When brilliant summer-time spreads its coloured mantle
> Sweet-tasting fragrance!

Pignuts, wild marjoram, green leeks,
Verdant pureness.

Swarms of bees and chafers, the little musicians of the
world,
A gentle chorus:
Wild geese and ducks, shortly before summer's end,
The music of the dark torrent.

Fair white birds come, herons, seagulls,
The cuckoo sings between—
No mournful music! dun heathpoults
Out of the russet heather.

The voice of the wind against the branchy wood
Upon the deep-blue sky;
Falls of the river, the note of the swan,
Delicious music.

Without an hour of fighting, without the din of strife
In my house,
Grateful to the Prince who giveth every good
To me in my shieling.

Guare. I would give my glorious kingship
With the share of my father's heritage—
To the hour of my death I would forfeit it
To be in thy company, my Marvan.

Synge's kinship in this experience is not limited to his fellow countrymen of the great period of Irish civilization and poetry; it is shared at different points by nature poets of all times. It is an essential part of Synge's objective and dramatic nature that he makes no philosophic inferences from it.[7] Indeed it is, as we saw at the outset, the peculiar characteristic of Synge that he is at once a nature-mystic and a dramatist, that the two things are one in him, as perhaps in no other poet before him, that each, that is, is revealed in terms of the other, nature in terms of man's character, thought and fate, and man himself in great part in terms of his relations with nature.

[7] Nor does he, in the plays, make any explicit statement on the relationship which he continually indicates. In the two prose volumes, on the other hand, he shows that his awareness was also conscious and critical, describing the experience and interpreting the characters of the islanders in the light of it.

That he was able to do this depended almost entirely upon Synge's discovering in the world of his own day people whose experience was like his and who could become the stuff of drama. That is why Yeats's lines quoted at the head of this chapter seem to me the fittest summary of the processes and the materials out of which Synge's drama was made. No one who has considered his record of nature and man's relations to it can doubt that side of his experience, no one who has felt the power and ease of movement through action, character, and speech can doubt that the instinct of the dramatist was as strong in him as in the major Jacobeans. Yet it was a paradoxical combination and it was no less than a miracle that he found—perhaps by his own, perhaps through Yeats's perception of his need—the race of people who were themselves the inheritors of the original Irish worship of nature.

What Synge made of this material is known throughout the English-speaking world. *Riders to the Sea* and *The Playboy of the Western World* are played wherever Irish drama is known, and *Deirdre,* especially the last act, which is the only part he left in finished form, is read wherever tragic poetry is honoured. His development as a dramatist is swift. Scope and humour broaden and deepen successively from play to play; structural subtlety and irony define more and more clearly the grim, the parodoxical and the tragic implications of life. Yet at no time was he uncertain, and if *The Shadow of the Glen* is slighter, as I think it is, than any part of the last two he wrote, it is already clear and complete as a play. His tragedies are untouched by comedy; relief, in them, comes, as with the Greeks, in poetry, and the relief of poetic thought grows more comprehensive as we go from the hard condensation of the early *Riders to the Sea* to the wide and sunny beauty of *Deirdre.* But his comedies are either a frank mixture of the two elements or such laughter as trembles always on the verge of tragedy, and the intimacy of the blending becomes subtler, more bewildering, as we go from the simple contrasts and balances of *The Shadow of the Glen* through *The Well of the Saints* and *The Tinker's Wedding* to *The Playboy of the Western World.* There is at work a watchful mind, slowly observant, grave and capacious. It is never didactic, never abstract, never philosophical, yet full of that intent vigilance which science and tragedy share. It is concrete and dramatic; it works through the human individuals of its creating whose experience is yet universal, and values above all else the inwardness and individuality of that experience.

Because of this steady progression through the six years of Synge's career, it is probably *The Playboy* that shows his dramatic power at its ripest; for *Deirdre,* left unfinished at his death, lacks the final shaping. But the earlier play is a triumphant consummation of the form, perhaps essentially Irish in its material and so in its shape, which subsidiarizes event and takes for its main theme the growth of fantasy in a mind or a group of minds. It is often described by English audiences as "nothing but talk," and this (which they do not necessarily mean as depreciation) seems true if we compare it with much English comedy, in which character, event, and situation interlock and react upon each other; for here character is sometimes no more than the necessary foundation upon which situation can be built and dialogue as much occupied with the service of event and situation as with the revelation of character. If we compare *The Playboy* with a fair, representative comedy by Lyly, Chapman, Ben Jonson, Middleton, Marston, Fletcher, Congreve, Sheridan, Pinero, or Galsworthy, this becomes clear. For the new Irish comedy of the early twentieth century does something which might else seem only possible to a certain kind of psychological tragedy (such as Ibsen's *John Gabriel Borkman*); it dispenses with all but the minimum of outward event and takes for its theme a mind's exploration and discovery of itself. This, which can carry weight and even passion when the events are tragic, is by no means easy in comedy and except in the comedy of Irish life, where the "incorrigible genius for myth-making" provides its material, it is liable to relapse into revelation by event. Continuous self-revelation is only possible in comedy where the characters all have a natural tendency to find the processes of their own and other people's minds of absorbing interest, an astounding succession of shocks—"What business would the people here have but to be minding one another's business?" Mrs. Tarpey is right; this is the essential pre-supposition. From this characteristic of the dramatist's originals comes not only that comic, poetic imagery and description which is the main substance of Lady Gregory's shorter plays, but that delighted exploration of his own unfolding personality which Christy Mahon pursues breathlessly

through *The Playboy*. Moreover, the central figure can rely upon the equally delighted co-operation of a society of fantasy-builders as expert and as fruitful as himself, whether in the construction of the tale of catastrophic conflicts between Bartley Fallon and Red Jack Smith or in the creation of a hitherto nonexistent Christopher Mahon. And here Synge, both in *The Well of the Saints* and in *The Playboy,* advances upon Lady Gregory, who was the originator of this kind of comedy; he sees that the genius for myth-making finds its supreme expression in creating the most satisfying myth of all, that of personality. The substance and scope of his comedies at once becomes greater than hers and he can create a full length play out of that very habit which, when used to create only a myth of event, runs to no more than one act.

The form of *The Playboy,* then, its succession of conversations and narrations (slenderly interspersed with episodes) which leads up to the double reversal of the climax, comes directly from its main theme, the growth, like a Japanese paper flower dropped into a bowl of water, of Christopher Mahon's new self.

His evolution from what his father brutally but succinctly describes as a dribbling idiot, not merely into "a likely man," but into a poet-hero, "the only playboy of the western world," is rapid but sure. So sure that when the reversal comes the new Christy is capable of ousting the original and perpetuating itself. It is the favouring atmosphere of a world of fantasy-builders that starts the process, a world in which whatever is unknown is presumed to be magical and where no talker is without honour, provided he has the luck or sense not to carry on his craft in his own country. Christy creeps into Flaherty's inn and the fostering warmth is enough. The "polis" never come there; "it is a safe house, so," and the crime for which he had fled in terror on the roads of Ireland since "Tuesday was a week," becomes "maybe something big." The mystery quickens the blood of his audience, they "draw nearer with delighted curiosity" and, looking into his own mind for the first time by the illumination of this tribute to his art, he perceives that there is not "any person, gentle, simple, judge or jury, did the like of me." From that moment a glorious and brilliant magnification of his deed and his situation sets in, he has "prison behind him, and hanging before, and hell's gap gaping below." Once the confession is out his audience contributes royally. They perceive that he is no "common, week-day kind of a murderer," but a man "should be a great terror when his temper's roused" and "a close man" into the bargain. (In fact, a complete Machiavellian, lion and fox together.) As the legend expands at the hands of his audience he accepts the additions, assimilating them so rapidly that they soon become part of his own memory of the event. With becoming modesty he gives the glory to God, but soon realizes that, "up to the day I killed my father there wasn't a person in Ireland knew the kind I was, and I there drinking, waking, eating, sleeping, a quiet, simple poor fellow with no man giving me heed." Before the evening is out the window Quinn has completed the first stage of his development; "It's great luck and company I've won me in the end of time—two fine women fighting for the likes of me—till I'm thinking this night wasn't I a foolish fellow not to kill my father in the years gone by."

In the second act the blossoming begins, to pass rapidly on to the fruits of confidence in Christy's victory at the sports at the beginning of the third act: "Didn't I know rightly I was handsome, though it was the divil's own mirror we had beyond, would twist a squint across an angel's brow." Christy enters upon a romantic career of bardic self-glorification. Each time he tells his story ("and if it was not altogether the same, anyway it was no less than the first story") he gathers in adroitly whatever had been contributed to the saga by each preceding audience. It is "a grand story," and "he tells it lovely." Honor's comment is true; whichever of his two antithetical selves Christy is at bottom, he is always a fine dramatic raconteur; herein lies his power of convincing himself and giving conviction, of sinking utterly into the myth that he is acting. In the love scenes with Pegeen he sorts the somewhat conflicting elements in his memory, rationalizing and explaining away the old Christy until finally, after the victory at the sports has given him incontestable proof, he grasps the new self so powerfully that it cannot be shaken even by the father he has dreaded all his life. "I'm master of all fights from now." He acknowledges the part his admiring audience has played, and whether it has contributed to self-realization, as he thinks, or to the expansion of a superb fantasy, as we half suppose, matters little, "for you've turned me a likely gaffer in the end of all, the way I'll go romancing through a romping life-time from this hour to the dawning of the judgment day."

The audience, led by Pegeen, with a reaction common to most romancers when romance presents itself on their doorstep, draw back in horror from the killing which they had glorified so long as it happened in "a windy corner of high, distant hills." They have learnt, for the moment, "that there's a great gap between a gallows story and a dirty deed." But Pegeen at least is won round at the last, for, after all, what she (and indeed all of them) has loved has been not so much the deed but the man "that has such poet's talking, and such bravery of heart." Beside this gift, with its power to bring glory and stir into a world of bog and stone, dirty shebeens and drunken wakes, little else matters. Any other man, beside Christy, is but "a middling kind of a scarecrow with no savagery or fine words in him at all." It is Synge's supreme skill in mixing the elements of comedy and tragic irony that leaves us at the end understanding not only how the hero-myth has been created but why. It is not Christy only, but the whole population of the small community he lights upon that has gone "romancing through a romping life-time," at least for the space of two days. The starved imaginations have made themselves drunk on fantasy as an alternative (or accompaniment) to the "flows of drink" at Kate Cassidy's wake, and when the curtain falls on the dreary public bar and the dishevelled, half-drunk men, we see what Pegeen and they have lost in the man "who'd capsize the stars." The life, aspirations and frustration of a whole country-side is in the play. . . .

A Player's Reflections on *Playboy*

by Cyril Cusack

I write primarily as an actor, which must at once set up a suspicion that what I say will be considerably coloured with ego and possible bias. So be it: I write out of my experience of playing Synge, and in particular the role of Christopher Mahon, which I have played over a period of just on twenty years—from 1936 to 1955—ranging from Dublin, through the Irish provinces, to London and Paris. It is the one of all his characters through which, to my mind, almost to the point of identification a player may reach closest to the essential Synge, the playwright in search of himself.

When first I joined the Abbey Theatre, at its old Marlborough Street house, in 1932, the Synge repertoire was staling into a collection of museum pieces. No longer did *The Playboy of the Western World* conjure up a popular reaction of any kind. (I can recollect only a sentimental salute of applause for the love-scene—at the height of the tourist season.) Its audiences sat, thin and depressingly inert, present, as it were, behind a stifled yawn, some from a dutiful habit of play-going, some out of academic or literary interest, others from sentiment or curiosity—a wordless contradiction of the wordy tales of riots and ructions in the Abbey's early years.

Within the Theatre itself, however, amongst both directors and players *Playboy* still could arouse enthusiasm, occasionally even tempers, but referring mainly to the manner in which the play should be presented and acted, rather as if they were holding up the mirror to some far glory that was past. Introduced as 'prentice-player to the Synge drama I was at once made aware it required a "tradi-

"A Player's Reflections on Playboy*" by Cyril Cusack. From* Modern Drama, *IV (December, 1961), 300–305. Copyright December 15, 1961, A. C. Edwards. Reprinted by permission of A. C. Edwards, Editor.*

tional" style of acting, with a strong insistence from the "traditionalists" on special rhythms and emphases in speech-delivery. It is true to say that already there existed in the Abbey, though a comparatively young theatre in the history of drama, a sense of tradition, but there was a tendency with some to hug it to death, forgetful of the fact that tradition, in order to remain vital, must draw upon the present as well as from the past. I approached my initiation with all due reverence.

Having myself, as a child-actor, emerged from the school of melodrama associated with Boucicault and the despised "stage-Irishman" —which, from Lady Gregory's pronunciamento, the Abbey was pledged to replace with indigenous theatre—I recognised the true theatrical quality of Synge. At the same time, instinctively I felt the necessity of relating the work to reality—as I knew it—and what I then understood as "reality" was drawn from my observation of Irish speech and character through a touring childhood. So, though I was ignorant of the fact that the dramatist had, as he tells us, composed his dialogue in phrases culled directly from the mouths of the people, without being fully conscious of what I was doing I set out to play in a "style" compounded of the purely theatrical with a form of naturalism perilously near to being simply representational, two apparently conflicting elements which nevertheless are present and compatible in the work of Synge. Needless to say, there was no great novelty in this, as I was to discover in my subsequent association abroad with many of the first generation Abbey players, of whose work in exile, even through an overlay of commercial theatre, I have had privileged glimpses; I would see that already had been achieved that fine balance of naturalism with the theatrical which was the ideal of Irish acting but which had fallen away, on the one hand into the near vaudevillian method demanded of the Irish actor by foreign commercial managements, and, on the other, into the false convention contrived by some of the later resident disciples of the Abbey tradition, or the pseudo-naturalism, later still, of younger reactionaries.

With the early disappearance from the Irish stage of Frank and W. G. Fay, who might be termed the Theatre's actor-founders, and —because of aims and views conflicting with those of its literary founders—with the general exodus from Ireland of such as Kerrigan and Digges, who left for America, and Sinclair, O'Rorke, Maire O'Neill and Sarah Allgood, who went to Britain, the unity of the company was temporarily broken and the acting tradition, so early flowering, was interrupted. Notwithstanding the arrival of individually great actors, like Barry Fitzgerald and F. J. McCormack, the succeeding company, though eventually an effective team, as a unit of personalities was less colourful. I should add that, while throughout its short history a number of highly competent and versatile players has remained with the Theatre, the general quality of the company has, however, from time to time taken on a different tone and emphasis.

My period with the Abbey Theatre, from 1932 to 1945, lay somewhere midways between the second group and the arrival of what I might describe as the Theatre's Gaelic-speaking era under the management of Mr. Ernest Blythe. From then on, many of the players were recruited from rural Ireland, instead of, as had occurred heretofore, from Dublin; and for a time this latest period bore the bruise of crude behaviourism on the stage. Happily, there are signs now of some artistic rejuvenescence.

To return to my early experience: while allowances were made by the "traditionalists" for my tentative and more exploratory renderings of Synge in some of the smaller roles—Bartley in "Riders to the Sea," Owen in *Deirdre of the Sorrows,* even the Tramp in "In the Shadow of the Glen"—when it came for me to play the major roles, of Christy in *The Playboy of the Western World* and Martin Doul in *The Well of the Saints,* murmurings were heard. On the opening night of a revival of the former play, with special settings and costume designs by the artist, Sean Keating, the late F. R. Higgins, poet and, at the time, managing-director of the Theatre, came to my dressing-room in a state of indignation:

"No Mayo man ever spoke like that!" he said.

"Why would he speak like a Mayo man?" I asked, in some bewilderment. "Isn't he from Kerry? Doesn't he say . . . 'I'm thinking Satan hasn't many have killed their da in Kerry and in Mayo too.'?"

Contrarily, the objection was concerned not so much with authenticity of dialect or the character's whereabouts as with the fact that in speaking the speech "trippingly on the tongue" I had broken with a convention, one which, to my way of thinking, had set a manner of delivery altogether remote from human communication; much as that which, in style of speech, stance, and movement, down to the slightest inflection, the smallest gesture—until revitalized by the modern approach—had mummified the Shakespearean theatre. My heresy hunted out, I pleaded, defending a rather open position, that never had I heard human being speak so, as this convention demanded, and I disclaimed it as alien to both author and audience. To my relief, the performance was generally accepted as a revival in the literal sense and thence forward I saw myself as a protagonist of Synge, with a responsibility to communicate his language to the audience as living speech.

At this point, let me allude to the fact that the literary group headed by W. B. Yeats and Lady Gregory which controlled, directed, and, indeed, inspired the Abbey Theatre, was of Anglo-Irish Protestant stock. Self-elected cultural leaders, they were properly regarded as such; yet, however idealistically motivated, as interpreters of the native genius they were not in true alignment with it. Synge, of similar stock but apart—the Irishman refound in France, Europeanized—penetrated more deeply into the character of the Gael; and, had he lived longer, with that sensitive ear he might have heard underneath the vivid phrases he recorded so assiduously and wove into multi-coloured theatre-designs, the full heart-beat of his people; in revealing more completely and universally its spiritual depths he might indeed have reached the full extent of his own rapidly maturing genius.

From this source, of the Anglo-Irish Literary Renaissance, stemmed the many pronouncements, manifestos, and theories setting forth the conditions of presenting Irish life and character on the stage; and for certain plays—it seems under special poetic licence—artificial rhythms, sounded too far from life to be wholly artistic, were conducted along on a depressingly incantatory note to substitute for the spontaneous poetry of normal native speech. At best, there was an over-emphasis—counteracted to a certain extent by the character-actors—a stress on the value of the spoken word at some expense to the universal dramatic situation. Another convention too much dwelt upon, particularly in retrospect, was that which, where there was speech, insisted on little or no movement from any quarter of the stage, or, at most, that dialogue follow on movement, movement on dialogue, a process which in itself could fracture the harmony of theatre. One could see the intention as being good and opposed to distraction, but it too could call up a fetish effecting in the actor a removal from life, and a woodenness and fear of reaction preventing awareness of the poetry of movement essential to complete theatre. The seed of life was stifled in an overgrowth of convention planted by the poetic ego for its own protection, and bored audiences looked for sustenance to the spurious manna of behaviourist comedy, with which soon the Irish stage, as with stages elsewhere, was to be deluged.

From my first playing of Christopher Mahon, which, erring on the side of naturalism, I related to myself, I became aware, as the play draws further away from the area of comedy towards its very much less comedic denouement, of some inadequacy, which for many years I attributed to the performance. Only latterly have I formed the opinion, however much it may smack of actor's vanity, that the inadequacy is in the play itself. This becomes evident as, with recurring anti-climax, it moves to its ending. Anti-climax is in the air when Christy, having chased Old Mahon with the loy, returns to the kitchen, alone, to be joined in a moment by Widow Quin who, with the girls, vainly tries to effect his escape. Again he is alone. (In the production with my company both in Dublin and Paris I had Christy flee the stage leaving it bare for the entry of the men.) Later comes the reentry of Old Mahon, "coming to be killed a third time . . ."; at the last there is Playboy's speech after which, by the author's direction, "he goes out," no more—a speech which, however rendered, only tolls a bell for the dead.

Christy, moving through a world of make-believe in which his listeners indulge with relish, reaches towards reality and self-discovery; as they accept, so he accepts his story, only here and there touching it with the shadow of positive mendacity; he assumes its central character as an actor identifying himself with the part he plays; but, unfortunately, at the play's ending reality disappears in a balloon-burst of disillusionment and the person of Christopher Mahon suddenly resolves itself into a dew. It is here that, as an actor, I find the part less than satisfying; here, where the playwright in search of himself is confronted with a void which is made the play's resolution. It is liberation, but a false one, of the artist in flight from reality; whom again we are invited to pursue into the mists in "In the Shadow of the Glen" and *The Well of the Saints.* This may be acceptable as a poetic reality within the experience of the playwright but it falls short of universality. Synge, dying so young, had not absorbed fully into his work the nature of the Irish people—only so much as could accommodate his quickening genius; perhaps it was for this reason he did not reach full maturity as a universal dramatist. Nevertheless, in his craftsmanship, in his sense of theatre, in his imagination and observation, in his desire and striving for identification with reality Synge is the greatest of the Irish dramatists.

Says the Philosopher in *The Crock of Gold,* "The end lies concealed in the beginning. . . ." About two years ago, at the suggestion of one of Synge's relatives, I requested Mrs. E. M. Stephens, his nephew's widow, to let me read an early unpublished play written by Synge when he was very young indeed. I was permitted to do so but not to take the manuscript away; I might read it but only within the precincts of the house. The play, which had no title, tells in two acts the story of the young Irish intellectual cast up on his native shore by the current *nouvelle vague* from France, and through this character, faintly foreshadowing "In the Shadow of the Glen," reveals Synge as knight-errant bent on liberating a nun from the toils of conventual life. Although written in an excessively literary style, with long quotations in French from the intellectuals he admired, it is revealing of the sensitive mind, the poetic imagination, above all the sense of dramatic atmosphere he infused into his later plays; it further suggests—but through the menial characters only—the style of speech which was to burgeon out in the flaming language of *Playboy.*

Synge, in all his plays, offers an artistic challenge to the actor. Here I must admit that I found myself constricted in the later Abbey form of presentation, and it was not until 1954, when I brought *The Playboy of the Western World* away from its old habitat and into a larger Dublin theatre, and once more out of the too naturalistic style I had helped to foster, into a wider acting orbit nearer to extravaganza, that as a player I came to enjoy the full flavour of this, Synge's best-known work. My almost piratical adventure with my company met acclaim both at home and abroad, which was not diminished in a subsequent tour of the Irish provinces, into towns where the play had not been seen in the half-century of its existence. Rather it received a fresh stimulus through these new audiences, lively, intelligent, appreciative and critical, and, I might add, less provincial—in the snobbish sense—than the frequently pseudo-sophisticated metropolitan audience.

Perhaps my greatest satisfaction with the play was during the first International Theatre Festival in Paris when, with my company, I presented it at the Sarah Bernhardt Theatre. It was accounted one of the two major contributions to the Festival, the other being Brecht's production of *Mutter Courage.* Here I dare to suggest that *Playboy* in Paris found its true home and audience. After all, did not the author once live but a few paces from the Odeon?

PART TWO

Several Sides of The Playboy

The Playboy of the Western World

by T. R. Henn

I

The Playboy does not lend itself readily to classifications; as we revolve it in our hands many facets take light and fire. In one mood we may suggest that it is sheer extravagant comedy, with elements of strong farce in the "resurrection" of Christy Mahon's father, and in the deflation of the boastful man, the revelation of a massive and mock-heroic lie. As such, it embodies the classic elements of reversal and recognition. Yet it is comedy that might have ended (for we are prepared from the first for a possible wedding) with Pegeen winning her Playboy and Old Mahon marrying the Widow Quin; comedy which at the end is edged, skilfully and unexpectedly, into a semi-tragedy. From another point of view we may call it "free" comedy, in which moral issues are reversed, transcended or ignored in the desire for "energy," though this view will be only part of the truth. It is helpful to quote Yeats:[1]

---

[1] *Explorations* (1962), pp. 161–2. This was a frequent thought: cf. "The Stare's Nest by My Window" (*Collected Poems* [1950], p. 230).

> We had fed the heart on fantasies,
> The heart's grown brutal from the fare:
> *More substance in our enmities*
> *Than in our love . . .*

> In a country like Ireland, where personifications have taken the place of life, men have more hate than love, for the unhuman is nearly the same as the inhuman, but literature, which is a part of that charity that is the forgiveness of sins, will make us understand men however little they conform to our expectations. We will be more interested in heroic men than in heroic actions, and will have a little distrust for everything that can be called good or bad in itself with a very confident heart.

Again we may see *The Playboy* (carrying Yeats' thought a stage further) as a Dionysiac comedy, in which the instincts are, within Synge's conventions, given uninhibited play; this in keeping with his demand for what is "superb and wild in reality." So the Playboy himself becomes a country Don Juan, rejoicing in his new-found power to excite the admiration of women,[2] and the very growth of the language, "richly flavoured as a nut or an apple," reflects his desire for "an imagination that is fiery and magnificent and tender."

We turn the play on its axis, and satire seems to predominate. It is a satire (but with more than a hint of approval) on the proverbial willingness of the West to give shelter to the malefactor and murderer, which goes back to the Elizabethan wars of conquest, the shipwrecked sailors of the Armada, and beyond. Then the Playboy may become a comic Oedipus, "the man who killed his da"; the mutual descriptions of each other by father and son give some point to the classic situation. There is satire in the pursuit of man by woman, the comic reversal of the conventional view; we may remember how Shakespeare and Shaw turned that theme to account, and the additional flavour lent to it by the romantically fostered idea of modest Irish womanhood. Indeed, we may carry the idea of the mock-heroic still further, and see in Christy Mahon an Odysseus, the wanderer cast up and seeking refuge; his triumph in the sports on the sea-shore a parody of the Greek games. We might then have a tragicomic piece with the Widow Quin as Nausicaa, a chorus of girls, the village pub for a palace. But again we may see it, if we will, as tragedy. The Playboy finds his soul through a lie,

[2] We may remember Othello's reported wooing of Desdemona: "Mark with what violence she loved the Moor but for bragging and telling her fantastical lies . . ."

the "gallous story" of his parricide. Under the stimulus of heady admiration from men and women he grows in stature and in poetry. Detail is elaborate, the fatal blow struck by the potato-spade (we may note the irony)[3] becomes more final, more heroic.[4] He is indeed of the company of poets, "fine fiery fellows with great rages when their temper's roused." Under the shock of his father's reappearance (and the old man's account of his son's character has prepared the audience for this) he staggers, weakens, and is finally reconciled; though with a new certainty of himself. He is "master of all fights from now." His father accepts the situation: "Glory be to God!" (*with a broad smile*) "I am crazy again." The final "turn" reminds us of the end of *The Shadow*: "By the will of God, we'll have peace now for our drinks." But it is Pegeen who is the heroine-victim. She has found her man, made him, won him in the teeth of opposition from her own sex. The marriage has been approved, in a superb drunken half-parody of the traditional blessing, by her father. From that marriage would come, because of Christy's heroic and virile virtues which have grown, mushroom-like, out of the tale of parricide, a band of "little gallant swearers by the name of God." At the end Pegeen's loss is absolute, beyond comfort, for she has lost her illusion of greatness in her man, and his body too; the complacent Shawn has seen the obstacle to his marriage removed.

> Oh my grief, I've lost him surely. I've lost the only Playboy of the Western World.

II

Synge intended that the play should run its course between antinomies. It is, for all its apparent simplicity of plot, a delicately balanced system of ironies, ambivalences, both of words and situation. We may quote his letter to the press after the storm of abuse which its production aroused:

[3] There may even be an echo of a once-popular song, "The Kerry Recruit": "So I buttered me brogues, and shook hands with me spade."

[4] Compare as stages in the narration: "I just riz the loy and let fall the edge of it on the ridge of his skull." ". . . the way they'd set their eyes upon a gallant orphan cleft his father with one blow to the breeches belt."

> *The Playboy* is not a play with a "purpose" in the modern sense of the word,

(he is thinking perhaps of Shaw, Brieux, and the then current misrepresentations of Ibsen as a didactic dramatist)

> —but, although parts of it are or are meant to be extravagant comedy, still a great deal that is in it and a great deal more that is behind it is perfectly serious when looked at in a certain light. This is often the case, I think, with comedy, and no one is quite sure today whether Shylock or Alceste should be played seriously or not. There are, it may be hinted, several sides to *The Playboy*.[5]

We may examine first the direct consequences of these "several sides" of the play. Synge's conflict with outraged Irish morality had begun as early as 1903, when the portrait of Nora in *The Shadow* was felt to be a slur on Irish womanhood. But the week that followed the first production of *The Playboy* on 26 January 1907 was a continuous riot, with a hysteria that recalls the first production of Victor Hugo's *Hernani* (with its violation of the formal Alexandrine) or the reception of Ibsen's *Ghosts* in London. We may quote from Lady Gregory:

> There was a battle of a week. Every night protestors with their trumpets came and raised a din. Every night the police carried some of them off to the police courts. Every afternoon the paper gave reports of the trial before a magistrate who had not heard or read the play and who insisted on being given details of its incidents by the accused and by the police . . . There was a very large audience on the first night . . . Synge was there, but Mr Yeats was giving a lecture in Scotland. The first act got its applause, and the second, though one felt that the audience were a little puzzled, a little shocked at the wild language. Near the end of the third act there was some hissing. We had sent a telegram to Mr Yeats after the end of the first act "Play great success"; but at the end we sent another —"Audience broke up in disorder at the word shift." [6]

We may attempt first to set out the main causes of offence, however innocent they may appear to a modern audience. As a background it is well to remember the image of Romantic Ireland, sedulously

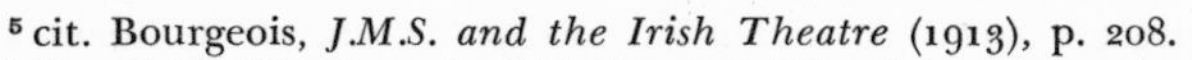

[5] cit. Bourgeois, *J.M.S. and the Irish Theatre* (1913), p. 208.

[6] *Our Irish Theatre,* cit. Ellis-Fermor, *The Irish Dramatic Movement,* p. 50.

fostered in the 90's: the Land of Saints, the country whose Literary Renaissance would save European culture. Ireland was the home of the most ancient Christian tradition; her women were models of chastity and purity. Against this are to be set the "heroic" aspects of homicide, countless jests on the subject during the agrarian troubles,[7] the Phoenix Park murders, the raw material of the play itself:

> An old man on the Aran Islands told me the very tale on which *The Playboy* is founded, beginning with the words: "If any gentleman has done a crime we'll hide him. There was a gentleman that killed his father, and I had him in my own house six months till he got away to America." [8]

As for the "wild language," Lady Gregory and the actors[9] had indeed protested against its coarseness before the play was produced. But it was, at least overtly, an indelicacy rather than a blasphemy that triggered off the riot:

> . . . a drift of chosen females, standing in their shifts itself, maybe, from this place to the eastern world.

The rancour of the mob centres on the fatal *shift;* in an access of outraged modesty, Victorian in character, but connected somehow with the idea that the very word was insulting to the womanhood of Ireland, whose chastity and purity had become a national myth, even as the saintliness of the island as a whole. It is probable that the audience, in their bewilderment at the more subtle ironies of the play, missed the full point of the phrase. The picture of Mayo maidens perceived in terms of a slave market, or a throng of Eastern houris, is made yet more fantastic in that the term *drift* is applied

[7] A shot fired in the dusk might provoke the hoary joke: "There goes another landlord"; and there were times when one did not sit between the window and a lamp. See, e.g., Lady Gregory's *Journals*.

[8] Yeats, *Essays and Introductions,* pp. 337–8. Synge's own version is in *The Aran Islands* (1907), pp. 64–5, together with some interesting aspects of the morality of this action.

[9] "Synge has just had an operation on his throat and has come through it all right. . . . When he woke out of the ether sleep his first words, to the great delight of the doctor, who knows his plays, were: 'May God damn the English, they can't even swear without vulgarity.' This tale delights the Company, who shudder at the bad language they have to speak in his plays" (Yeats, *Letters,* ed. Wade, p. 496). See also *Our Irish Theatre,* p. 133.

to a drove of heifers; and it is possible that they took the point of the *eastern* world (Leinster or Dublin) as opposed to the Western of Connemara or Mayo.

We may quote some of Yeats' account of the attacks on "this wild, laughing thing":

> Picturesque, poetical, fantastical, a masterpiece of style and of music, the supreme work of our dialect theatre, his *Playboy* roused the populace to fury. We played it under police protection, seventy police in the theatre the last night, and five hundred, some newspaper said, keeping order in the streets outside. It is never played before any Irish audience for the first time without something or other being flung at the players. In New York a currant cake and a watch were flung, the owner of the watch claiming it at the stagedoor afterwards. The Dublin audience has, however, long since accepted the play.[10]

And again:

> The Irish nationalists in America mobilized every force they could touch to boycott the [Abbey] plays throughout the Eastern States. The fight took much the same form everywhere, though it was fiercer in some towns than in others. It started in a prejudice, not the less violent for its ignorance and generally among the members of the Gaelic League, against the picture of Irish life and morals which the plays of the new school were said to give. The general prejudice was entangled with and sometimes manipulated by political prejudices of a far-reaching and almost infinitely complex kind. And mingled again with both was the religious prejudice of some sections at least of the Church.[11]

It seems to me likely that the offensive word was no more than a catalyst for the general but indeterminate unease caused by a number of other factors in the play; and these factors in this are themselves complicated by Synge's technique of producing, deliberately, an ebb and flow in the audience's response to character and situation.[12] The perception of ironies and ambivalences will, of course, vary with the type of audience, its age and its environment. It is worth noting, for example, that *The Playboy* was more popular in England, *The Shadow* in Ireland; and the Dublin audiences in

[10] *Autobiographies* (1955), p. 569. (This was written in 1925.)
[11] Ellis-Fermor, op. cit., p. 54.
[12] For an account of this, see J. L. Stayan, *The Elements of Drama,* p. 57 et. seq.

1907 might well have been particularly sensitive to anything provided by the "Anglo-Irish Ascendancy" group of writers.[13] The more subtle, dispassionate and balanced the irony the less likely it is that the general pattern will be perceived, and the more probable that overt points of conventional distaste will be selected for attack. In *The Tinker's Wedding* Synge pleaded, unavailingly, for the recognition of a humour without malice. That of *The Playboy,* fantastic as it may be, was probably too close to observation to be taken lightly.

Synge's attitude to Ireland and to the Irish peasantry was highly ambivalent: insight combined with toleration, love without passion. We may think of broadly similar positions taken up by Swift, Shaw, Yeats. Love and understanding are not inseparable from a detached mockery. But the union of these may be so subtle, so fluctuating and yet so integral to the whole system of values in the play, that we may examine briefly some of the instances.

His irony is founded most often on incongruity, the perception of polar opposites;[14] and within the broad rhythm of the play's construction, the manipulation of character so that it rises and falls, retreats and advances in the sympathy of the audience, to form its characteristic patterns. The irony may go unperceived, or be furiously rejected, when one of the poles from which the current passes is felt by the audience to be unacceptable; whether as involving religion, womanhood, King Lear's "nature," drunkenness, or aesthetic delicacy. (Curiously enough, the morbid, particularly of the churchyard, seems to go unchallenged; the accessories or instruments of death have a perennial attraction for a peasantry.)

It was a lady novelist of the early nineteenth century who noted the proclivity of the Irish for swearing, and on those somewhat tenuous grounds asserted the Grecian origin of the Milesians. "It is certain that the habit of confirming every assertion with an oath is

[13] We may reflect, for example, on the affair of the Municipal Gallery and Lutyens' plans, and the bitter poems in Yeats' *Responsibilities.* Behind it again was the doctrinal controversy over *The Countess Cathleen.*

[14] These "metaphysical" juxtapositions are everywhere, particularly when he wishes to emphasize the humanity of his characters: e.g. "I've a grand story of the great queens of Ireland, with white necks on them the like of Sarah Casey, and fine arms would hit you a slap the way Sarah Casey would hit you." "At your age you should know there are nights when a king like Conchubor would spit upon his arm ring, and queens will stick their tongues out at the rising moon."

as prevalent among the Irish as it was among the ancient, and is among the modern Greeks."[15] In the Notes to these plays I have drawn attention to some instances of a pleasant and at best devotional practice in this respect. But rapid and violent verbal conjunction may give quite another aspect. Consider, for instance:

> . . . or Marcus Quin, God rest him, got six months for maiming ewes—

("God rest him" is the normal pious expletive concerning the dead, but here a little incongruous with his crime)

> —and he a great warrant to tell stories of holy Ireland . . .

—where the second clause links "holy Ireland" with "God rest him," and both combine ironically with the "six months for maiming ewes." But set against this triangle there are two background references: to the Moonlighters and the agrarian troubles with their horrible practice of maiming cattle, horses, sheep by hamstringing or cutting off their tails. The second is to the juxtaposition of "holy Ireland," the kind of reference embodied in Yeats' poem whose title is the first three words:

> Beautiful lofty things: O'Leary's noble head;
> My father upon the Abbey stage, before him a raging crowd:
> "This Land of Saints," and then as the applause died out,
> "Of plaster Saints;" his beautiful mischievous head thrown back.[16]

Something of the same metaphysical conjunction (which emerges only when distanced) is in Shawn's agonized cry "Oh, Father Reilly and the saints of God, where will I hide myself today?" Sometimes we have a double counterpointing, when the romantic, the religious, and the realistic meet in a vortex characteristic of Synge's technique:

> Amn't I after seeing the love-light of the star of knowledge shining from her brow, and hearing words would put you thinking on the holy Brigid speaking to the infant saints, and now she'll be turning again, and speaking hard words to me, like an old woman with a spavindy ass she'd have, urging on a hill.

or,

[15] Sydney Owenson, *The Wild Irish Girl.*
[16] *Collected Poems,* p. 348.

> There's poetry talk for a girl you'd see itching and scratching, and she with a stale stink of poteen on her from selling in the shop.

More subtle and less definable is Sara's speech as she tries on the boots:

> There's a pair do fit me well, and I'll be keeping them for walking to the priest, when you'd be ashamed this place, going up winter and summer with nothing worth while to confess at all.

—when the ideas of confession and barefoot penance have a kind of subtle and uneasy association. It is the same with the convolutions of the plot. *The Playboy*'s epic blow grows steadily in narration; but it is counterpointed and parodied by Pegeen's account of how the Widow Quin killed *her* man:

> She hit himself with a worn pick, and the rusted poison did corrode his blood the way he never overed it, and died after. That was a sneaky kind of murder did win small glory with the boys itself.

and yet again Pegeen's

> And to think of the coaxing glory we had given him, and he after doing nothing but hitting a soft blow and chasing northward in a sweat of fear.

There are the overt attacks on custom; the terrifying description of Kate Cassidy's wake is balanced against Michael's drunken blasphemy:

> . . . aren't you a louty schemer to go burying your poor father unbeknownst when you'd a right to throw him on the crupper of a Kerry mule and drive him westwards, *like holy Joseph in the days gone by,* the way we would have given him a decent burial, and not have him rotting beyond, *and not a Christian drinking a smart drop to the glory of his soul?* [17]

Now the uneasiness set up in an audience is caused, not by the extravagance of these syntactical conjunctions, but because each one of them is, *in itself,* perfectly natural and in common use, and is therefore elusive. It is Synge's art, which has something in com-

[17] See Notes on the wake in *The Shadow*.

mon with Pope's, of suggesting value or its depreciation in this manner. Much the same is true of the plot, with its fantastical propositions. Does murder become heroic just because the blow is a good one, or because it and its context are narrated poetically? Granted that the police, together with the "khaki cut-throats," are natural enemies of the community, embodying "the treachery of the law," is it a moral act to shelter wrong-doers? Is a murderer likely to be a proper protector for Pegeen while the others are out? Is his reported valour a sufficient counterweight to the impropriety of his being left alone with her? If women are so easily won by poetical speech combined with inferred virility, what is the position of the conventional timid man as represented by Shawn Keogh?

Old Mahon boasting of his drink and lechery, his treatment in hospital, is in some sense a counterpart to the boasting of his son. They go off together, united in an utter reversal of this relationship.

> Go with you, is it? I will then, like a gallant captain with his heathen slave.

and old Mahon's comment, that oblique and perhaps profound comment on metaphysics:

> Glory be to God! I am crazy again.

So Synge's art makes the characters and the themes advance and retreat from the audience. Outrageous statements become logical,[18] and the language of hyperbole makes them still more credible, in relation to the reality which is being questioned.

It is being questioned, of course, in the very title. A geographer could fix the scene of *The Playboy* with some accuracy. It is obviously in north-west Mayo, within sight of the sea-shore, and of the dominant mountain Nephin. It is not far from Belmullet and Castlebar. The Western World is the land lying westward of the Shannon; proverbial for its "wildness" and poverty; isolated from the civilized East and South, and the dour virtues of the "black North." Perhaps there are connotations of the Holy Islands, the Country of the Sunset, St. Brandon. Yet it is a *world,* fantastic,

[18] Perhaps this is the reason for the inclusion of *The Playboy* in the Surrealist Manifesto (Owen Quinn in *Envoy*).

romantic, brutal and sentimental, all at once. In the play Synge's own ambivalent attitude is fully apparent:

> I once said to John Synge, "Do you write out of love or hate for Ireland?" and he replied, "I have often asked myself that question . . ." [19]

Let us be frank about it. Synge's satiric view is constantly focused, with more or less directness, towards certain aspects of the peculiar blend of paganism and Roman Catholicism that he saw in the West. The pious ejaculations can, by juxtaposition and contrast, become loaded with ironies that demand both distance and an Anglo-Irish viewpoint to imagine their full implications. The unseen Father Reilly hovers in the background of *The Playboy* as the guardian of peasant morality, the supporter of the cowardly and feeble Shawn; whose comments on each situation are yet those of the ordinary moral man. Against settled and dull convention and a religion which can be made to appear superficial there are set Synge's tinkers, tramps, fishermen, publicans, in their actual or potential vitality. Yeats recognized the potential conflicts in a letter to Ricketts:

> I notice that when anybody here writes a play it always works out, whatever the ideas of the writer, into a cry for a more abundant and intense life. Synge and "AE" the poet are staying here, and though they have come to their task from the opposite sides of the heavens they are both stirring the same pot—something of a witches' cauldron, I think.[20]

The Playboy exists as a work of art, and in a sense all comments on it are futile or irrelevant. The complexity that gives it life must be apprehended with all our senses. Its verbal harmonies and disharmonies are integral with its verbal rhythms and idiom, its characters with the waves and currents of the plot. We stand back from it, and we may remember Shaw:

> . . . the admirable comedies of Synge, who, having escaped from Ireland to France, drew mankind in the manner of Molière, and discreetly assured the public that this was merely the human nature

[19] Yeats, *Letters,* ed. Wade, p. 618.
[20] ibid., p. 436.

of the Blasket Islands, and that, of course, civilized people never admired boastful criminals nor esteemed them according to the atrocities they pretended to commit. The Playboy's real name was Synge; and the famous libel on Ireland (and who is Ireland that she should not be libelled as other countries are by their great comedians?) was the truth about the world.[21]

[21] G. B. Shaw, *The Matter with Ireland,* p. 84.

Synge's *Playboy*: Morality and the Hero

by Norman Podhoretz

Synge's *The Playboy of the Western World* is a dramatic masterpiece. On this, it seems, there has been critical unanimity. Yeats, for example, called it "the strangest, the most beautiful expression in drama of that Irish fantasy which . . . is the unbroken character of Irish genius." But the critics have not been very helpful in explaining what makes the play a masterpiece. "It brought to the contemporary stage the most rich and copious store of character since Shakespeare," writes P. P. Howe, but he goes no further by way of interpretation than a summary of the plot. Yet that there is something to interpret should be obvious from even a casual glance at the plot, which clearly has the myth of rebellion against the father at its basis.

Christy, we are told, "kills" his father for two reasons: he is tired of being goaded on the score of his physical and sexual timidity, and, more immediately, he refuses to marry the old woman who had nursed him as a baby. The primitive people of Mayo (with whom Christy has taken refuge) not only refuse to give him up to the police, but make a hero of him instead. Encouraged by their admiration, Christy begins growing into manhood with full command of his physical and sexual powers. With the suggestion of the myth in mind, we can appreciate the significance of Christy's reception by the Mayoites. First of all, it must be noted that there is another "murderer" in the play who, like Christy, has escaped punishment but who is nevertheless despised in Mayo—the Widow Quin. Hers "was a sneaky kind of murder did win small glory with the boys itself." A more important

"Synge's Playboy: *Morality and the Hero" by Norman Podhoretz. From* Essays in Criticism, *III (July, 1953), 337–44. Reprinted by permission of F. W. Bateson, Editor.*

pointer is that the second time Christy "kills" his father, the Mayoites turn on him. Michael James, who had told Christy that "a daring fellow is the jewel of the world, and a man did split his father's middle with a single clout should have the bravery of ten, so may God and Mary and St. Patrick bless you and increase you from this mortal day," now invokes the curse of God against him: "If we took pity on you the Lord God, would, maybe bring us ruin from the law today." Obviously Synge knew what he was doing and meant us to understand that the Mayoites saw a great difference between the three murders. An examination of their reasons carries us to the heart of Synge's meaning.

The Mayoites are primitive people who live almost entirely in an imaginative world of their own creation. They are all poets *manqués;* their life is all language, and it is only what they can make poetry out of that is important to them. Pegeen's complaint that there is no material in "this place" for her imagination to work on is revealing:

> It's a wonder, Shaneen, the Holy Father'd be taking notice of the likes of you; for if I was him, I wouldn't bother with *this* place where you'll meet none but Red Linahan, has a squint in his eye, and Patcheen is lame in his heel, or the mad Mulrannies were driven from California and they lost in their wits.

It is no accident, then, that Christy who is, as will be seen, the undeveloped poet coming to consciousness of himself as man and as artist, should be accepted with such fervour. This was no ordinary, everyday murder he had committed, but an act of great "daring" such as the Mayoites have never had before their very eyes until this day. Moreover, they recognize that there was something heroic, something *necessary* about the deed, which makes the question of crime irrelevant. "Up to the day I killed my father," says Christy, "there wasn't a person in Ireland knew the kind I was, and I there drinking, waking, eating, sleeping, a quiet, simple poor fellow with no man giving me heed." And Pegeen answers: "It's near time a fine lad like you should have your good share of the earth." Consciousness, maturity, self-realization were bound up with revolt against the father, and Pegeen, with her sure earthy instinct, senses this.

Gradually Synge tells us more and more about the earlier Christy and his sexual timidity, which is characterized throughout in animal images:

> *Peg.* It was the girls were giving you heed, maybe . . .
> *Chr.* Not the girls itself, and I won't tell you a lie. There wasn't anyone heeding me in that place saving only the dumb beasts of the field.

Mahon, Christy's father, later confirms this, using almost identical imagery:

> If he had seen a red petticoat coming swinging over the hill, he'd be off to hide in the sticks, and you'd see him shooting out his sheep's eyes between the little twigs and the leaves, and his two ears rising like a hare looking out through a gap. Girls, indeed!

The results of Christy's revolt are what we should expect them to be: sexual assertion and a new awareness of self:

> *Peg.* Wasn't I telling you, and you a fine, handsome young fellow with a noble brow?
> *Chr.* (*with a flush of delighted surprise*) Is it me?
> *Peg.* Aye. Did you never hear that from the young girls where you come from in the west or south?
> *Chr.* (*with venom*) I did not, then. Oh, they're bloody liars in the naked parish where I grew a man.

And Christy's soliloquy at the end of Act I, when the forces have all been set in motion, is exact evidence of Synge's comic genius:

> Well, it's a clean bed and soft with it, and it's great luck and company I've won me in the end of time—two fine women fighting for the likes of me—till I'm thinking this night wasn't I a foolish fellow not to kill my father in the years gone by.

If we stop to analyse the humour of this passage, we see that it derives from an absurd moral position, and indeed, what Synge has grasped here is nothing less than the paradox on which civilization (according to the myth, at any rate) seems to rest—individual achievement and communal progress depend on murder. The moral consciousness has found a way out of the dilemma for civilized man: he commits a *symbolic* act of murder in place of physical violence by rejecting the father and his values, but in the primitive world of Act I there is as yet no sign of morality. Synge will begin to draw it into his play slowly in Act II, and it becomes so important to the dénouement that I will have to return to a discussion of the whole problem later. We cannot understand the climax of the play without appreciating Synge's profound sense of the relation between symbolism and morality.

The second reason for Christy's success in Mayo is, of course, his greatness as a poet. Indications of this are so numerous in the text that it would be difficult to quote them all, but several passages in which the theme is stressed are worth looking at. "I've heard all times," Pegeen says rhapsodically, "it's the poets are your like—fine, fiery fellows with great rages when their temper's roused." Again, when Christy has been boasting to the girls who come to pay homage to his heroism, and has been expanding his deed into epic proportions, Susan's only comment is, "That's a grand story," and Honor agrees, adding that "he tells it lovely." And finally, the Widow Quin (she senses more than she knows) snorts at one point, "There's poetry talk for a girl you'd see itching and scratching, and she with a stale stink of poteen on her from selling in the shop." Synge's dialogue, we may note in passing, is never irrelevantly lyrical: the quality of the language itself is organic to the play's meaning. Language is the very being of these people, and so they naturally pay tribute to the great master of language who has come among them. Moreover, it is the poetic, the symbolic deed which has set their imaginations afire: the murder has for them the reality of fitness and beauty but never the reality of fact. Christy, who is taken in by the poetic glory of what he has done no less than Pegeen, neglects to remember the harsh details:

> I just riz the loy and let fall the edge of it on the ridge of his skull, and he went down at my feet like an empty sack, and never let a groan or grunt from him at all.

The last phrase is enormously revealing: Christy has no notion of what he has done to his father; he cannot see the suffering his act has caused and he is not aware of its brutality, which is only a way of saying that he has no moral consciousness. And so with Pegeen; she will not allow Shawn to call Christy a "bloody handed murderer." That there should have been blood cannot occur to her, because the murder is "a gallous story," a symbolic event, an expression of what is fine in the human spirit. Christy had a right to kill his father; and more, it was necessary and good that he should do so.

They all regard the murder essentially in terms of its symbolic and imaginative overtones, and indeed, symbolic is precisely what the first murder turns out to be. The "old man of the tribe" has not been killed, and the fact that his appearance terrifies Christy tells us that the first murder was not so emancipating as it seemed. Still another act of violence is necessary if Christy is to triumph over his father, over, that is, those forces which have prevented the full emergence of his identity. And here the moral paradox of which I spoke above asserts itself most strongly. The original act represented the instinctive stirrings of manhood in Christy, while for the people of Mayo it was "a gallous story" rather than "a dirty deed." Christy, however, murders again not instinctively but deliberately, out of a desire to protect his newly-found independence:

> Shut your yelling (he says), for if you're after making a mighty man of me this day by the power of a lie, you're setting me now to think if it's a poor thing to be lonesome, it's worse, maybe, go mixing with the fools of earth.

This, of course, is a moral act, the result of a choice, and partly for that reason, the Mayoites now turn on Christy. The sight of blood makes them aware of the realities of suffering and murder, and Pegeen, at least, realizes how great a gap there is "between a gallous story and a dirty deed." From the point of view of society, the second murder is certainly a dirty deed; Pegeen's downfall is assured when she shows herself unable to consider it from any other point of view:

> Take him on from this, *for I think bad the world should see me* raging for a Munster liar, and the fool of men.
>
> (My italics)

But another valid point of view is presented—Christy's; he can see no real alternative to the second murder:

> And I must go back into my torment is it, or run off like a vagabond straying through the unions with the dust of August making mud-stains in the gullet of my throat; or the winds of March blowing on me till I'd take an oath I felt them making whistles of my ribs within?

Christy, then, makes a choice, but it remains to be noticed that he does so without knowledge of the consequences: Synge is careful to show that Christy had not believed his admirers would turn on him; his immediate motive for killing his father again is that they have taunted him with a lie. His absurd and magnificent willingness, however, to kill his father yet a third time ("Are you coming to be killed a third time, or what ails you now?") is the product of a full moral consciousness. He knows that they will hang him if he raises the loy once more, but the necessity of ultimate triumph is more important, is absolute. This finally establishes Christy as the Hero who has the courage to face up to that paradox on which civilization rests, who will commit the act of violence which all feel to be necessary and which society cannot afford to condone. And it is beautifully proper that Christy's triumph does not entail self-destruction. For Synge is telling us, I think, that the Hero, the poet who does in fact challenge morality with its own contradictions will not be destroyed, that he will be saved by a kind of Grace. There is, unfortunately, no other word (unless it be "luck") for the power which saves Christy and which resolves the dilemma lying at the heart of the play. And we should not be surprised at the invocation of the idea of Grace in a work so saturated with religious awareness. Synge's religion is not Father Reilly's, but it is a religion nonetheless. He believes (to borrow a phrase from Henry James) in the salubrity of genius: Christy is the poet, the playboy, triumphant in games, who will spend his life "romancing" and "telling stories" now that he has been made "a likely gaffer in the end of all." Society has not been able to countenance him and all he represents, and in the name of order and peace they have driven him out into "the lonesome west":

> *Mic.* By the will of God, we'll have peace now for our drinks. . . .
> *Sha.* It's a miracle Father Reilly can wed us in the end of all, and we'll have none to trouble us when his vicious bite is healed.

But nothing can heal Christy's "vicious bite" as far as Pegeen is concerned. She realizes when Christy leaves declaring that he is "master of all fights now" what she has lost, what the meaning of his strange salvation is, and she knows that she is consigned to a life in society with the likes of Shawn Keogh: "Oh, my grief, I've lost him surely. I've lost the only Playboy of the Western World."

A few remarks are necessary, finally, to clarify Synge's attitude towards society and the Hero. The charm with which he invests the people of Mayo, and the fact that he is constantly critical of Christy, are enough to dissociate Synge from the currently fashionable school of "alienationists"—he is not defending the frail artistic sensibility from the onslaughts of a morality that stunts the artist's growth. The Hero and society are incompatible in the sense that they pursue different objectives, but the relation between them must be understood as one of reciprocal benefit no less than of antagonism. Christy develops into a Hero only when the superior instinct of society approves what he had done in ignorance and bewilderment, and the Mayoites, on the other hand, move from a primitive state of consciousness to a sense of civilization and its values through their contact with him. The West is a lonesome place, Synge tells us early in the play, but Christy has made his choice: "If it's a poor thing to be lonesome, it's worse, maybe, go mixing with the fools of earth." What he has to do, Christy must do alone. Synge, then, is alive both to the possibilities of the Shawns and the Michael Jameses, and to the worth of the Christies, and his sympathy is patently divided between those two extremes. His pity, however, Synge reserves for Pegeen, who—to paraphrase Eliot—has been visited by the vision of greatness for a few days and will for ever after be a haunted woman. The tragic implications of *The Playboy of the Western World* are that the type represented by Pegeen—those who can perceive greatness but cannot rise to it, who are weighed down by the "society" within them—can neither live in the lonesome west playing out their days, nor be happy in the little world of daily preoccupations. The Christies are somehow taken care of, and so are the Shawns; it is the Pegeens who suffer most from the radical incompatibility of Hero and society.

The Making of the Playboy

by Patricia Meyer Spacks

Yeats said of *The Playboy of the Western World* that the inability of the original audiences to understand it represented the only serious failure of the Abbey Theatre movement.[1] The most recent significant appearance of *The Playboy* took place off-Broadway in 1958, and its reviewers, though generally kind, revealed, like those of the past, some confusion as to the essential import of the play. Indeed, *The Playboy* seems a work destined to be forever misinterpreted. At the start of its career in 1907 it caused riots because of its alleged immorality; since then it has produced mainly perplexity. Seeing a realistic production of *The Playboy,* one is made acutely conscious of the problem which Synge himself raised during the first tumultuous week of the original Dublin performance, when he insisted he'd written "an extravaganza"—only to add later that the source of the playboy lay in his understanding of Irish psyche and Irish speech as they actually existed, thus claiming for the work an ultimate realism.[2]

The dilemma of whether *The Playboy* is essentially realistic or fantastic is the one on which producers and critics have foundered ever since. Viewed as realistic drama, the play immediately begins to seem implausible. That a man should become to strangers a hero by virtue of a tale of patricide, and become in the end gen-

---

[1] W. B. Yeats, "On Taking *The Playboy* to London," *Plays and Controversies* (London, 1923), p. 197.

[2] See, for example, the detailed account of the play's early history in David H. Greene and Edward M. Stephens, *J. M. Synge* (New York, 1959), pp. 238–251.

uinely masterful for no readily apparent reason—the psychology of the real world is little help in interpreting these events. On the other hand, if one considers the play as fantasy, it begins to seem strangely random and undeniably hampered by its realistic elements. *The Playboy* has usually been admired for its quaintness, its poetry, or its comic force, and, though a popular anthology piece and reasonably often revived, has been universally underrated as a coherent work of art.[3] I do not plan a full reading of it here, but wish to trace a source of the play's power which has never been insisted upon by critics or producers.

One aspect of *The Playboy* that seems disturbing is the curious tone with which it treats the theme of patricide. To be sure, the second time Christy strikes his father the spectators on stage feel that he should be hanged for his deed. But they are in no way horrified by it: they believe Christy to be potentially dangerous to them and they fear legal involvement in his crime; self-preservation motivates them. Nor, for that matter, does the revived father appear to think that there is anything extraordinary about a son who has twice tried to kill him. He resents the attempts in a personal way —as well he might—but he does not find them unnatural. The emotional weight of *The Playboy of the Western World* is on patricide as a noble deed, not as an abhorrent one.

Oedipus kills his father, and the crime brings a plague on his city. Orestes kills his mother and is pursued by furies. Patricide and matricide were for sophisticated Greeks the most dreadful of sins; Freud has brought modern readers to consciousness of the roots of the horror which the Greeks felt, and which twentieth-century audiences of Greek tragedy continue to feel. Yet Synge somehow manages to treat so dreadful a theme with apparent lightness. For parallels to this sort of treatment, one must go to the folk tale. The pages of Grimm are full of violence: giants who

[3] Two recent critics have provided notable exceptions to this generalization. In "The Hero as Playboy," *University of Kansas City Review,* XXI (1954), 9–19, Hugh H. MacLean offers an interpretation of the play in which Christy is a Christian scapegoat who can only save himself, not the world. Closer to my reading is Norman Podhoretz's "Synge's *Playboy*: Morality and the Hero," *Essays in Criticism,* III (1953), 337–44. [Reprinted above, pp. 68–74.] Mr. Podhoretz sees Christy's "murders" as the symbolic self-assertions of the ultimately anti-social hero.

eat their victims, blood and bones; enchanters who turn the unwary to stone; kings who demand the impossible and cut off the heads of those who fail to achieve it. Irish folk tales, of course, deal with the same sort of material; their heroes wade through blood to prove themselves. To be sure, this violence has a somewhat factitious quality: one is always aware that those who are turned to stone will become flesh and blood again at the end; that the frog, once its head is cut off, will turn into a prince; that however many anonymous warriors are slaughtered along the way, the true hero will accomplish the impossible and not be slaughtered himself.

In *The Playboy,* too, extreme violence is in a sense unreal. Both "murders" take place off stage. Moreover, neither of them really takes place at all: twice the father, in effect, rises from the dead, as people rise from the dead in fairy tales. Yet the symbolic violence, as in a fairy tale, shapes and defines the story: without his attempts to murder his father, one cannot imagine Christy becoming a man. One finds the same sort of pattern in many folk tales. In "The Battle of the Birds," an Irish fairy tale for which parallels exist "throughout the Indo-European world," [4] the king's son has to undergo a series of tests before he can win Auburn Mary as a bride. Last of all, he must obtain five eggs from the top of a 500-foot tree. To get the eggs, Mary tells him, he must kill her, strip the flesh from her bones, take the bones apart, and use them as steps for climbing the tree. The prince is reluctant, but the girl insists; after the task is completed, she is rejuvenated from scattered bones and becomes his wife.[5] The murder of the girl, then, is totally unreal, yet it is absolutely essential for the hero's winning of her.

The necessity for violence in the process of testing and maturing is, of course, frequently emphasized in folk tales: it is for precisely this reason that some modern censors have doubted the suitability of such tales for children's reading. The hero must cut off, on three successive days, the three heads of the "Laidly Beast";[6] or he must fight first a giant with one head, then a giant with two heads,

[4] Joseph Jacobs, ed., *Celtic Fairy Tales* (New York, 1894), Notes and References, p. 265.

[5] "The Battle of the Birds," Jacobs, pp. 214–16.

[6] "The Sea-maiden," Jacobs, p. 144.

then a giant with three heads.[7] We feel that such obstacles are important mainly as tests, hindrances of increasing complexity and difficulty which must be overcome on the road to maturity. Ritual bloodshed is both necessary and significant: blood must be shed before the child becomes a man, before the non-entity becomes a hero.[8] And the strange attitude toward father-murder in *The Playboy* is explainable in exactly the same way. The frivolity with which the first murder is treated is justifiable on the ground that it never in actuality takes place: it is more obviously unreal than a fantasy of murdered giants. But more importantly, the attitude of the playwright toward the murder is justifiable because the murder itself is justifiable—and more than justifiable: even necessary. It is a ritual murder, a step in the process toward maturity.

Certainly there is no question that Christy grows before our very eyes in *The Playboy*. The frightened boy who comes on stage in the first act, looking nervously about him, asking if the police are likely to come, miserably gnawing a turnip before the fire, is quite different from the Christy who departs in the last act. He leaves the stage with these words: "Ten thousand blessings upon all that's here, for you've turned me a likely gaffer in the end of all, the way I'll go romancing through a romping lifetime from this hour to the dawning of the judgment day." He recognizes the change in himself, and blesses the tavern company for having brought it about. But the responsibility is his, not theirs, and the transformation has been accomplished through the successive murders of his father.

Characteristically in the folk tale, actions, tests, come in groups of three. The prince in "The Battle of the Birds" undergoes three tests; Conn-Eda, whose story is retold by Yeats, has to procure three magic objects;[9] the young gardener in "The Greek Princess and the Young Gardener" has to obtain not only the golden bird he first set out for, but also the King of Morocco's bay filly and the

[7] "The Lad with the Goat-Skin," Jacobs, p. 226.

[8] For an especially good example of this theme, see "The Tailor and the Three Beasts" in Douglas Hyde, ed., *Beside the Fire: A Collection of Irish Gaelic Folk Stories* (London, 1890), p. 2.

[9] "The Story of Conn-Eda; Or, the Golden Apples of Lough Erne," W. B. Yeats, ed., *Fairy and Folk Tales of the Irish Peasantry* (London, 1888), pp. 306–318.

daughter of the King of Greece.[10] In this play, too, there are three tests, three ritual murders, not merely two, and the development of Christy's character takes place through them. The Christy with whom the play begins is described by his father, in the boy's absence, as "a dirty, stuttering lout." Christy is, old Mahon continues, "a liar on walls, a talker of folly, a man you'd see stretched the half of the day in the brown ferns with his belly to the sun." He is lazy, frightened of girls, "a poor fellow would get drunk on the smell of a pint," with a "queer rotten stomach." He is the laughingstock of all women; the girls stop their weeding when he comes down the road and call him "the looney of Mahon's."

There is something familiar about this characterization: we have here the foolish son of so many fairy tales, the male equivalent of Cinderella. Sons, in folk tales, also usually appear in threes. Two of them are reputed to be clever and brave, but they fail when they undertake the crucial quest. The youngest son is scorned by all, thought unworthy even to attempt the quest, considered foolish and stupid and cowardly, the one least likely to succeed. "A poor woman had three sons. The eldest and second eldest were cunning clever fellows, but they called the youngest Jack the Fool, because they thought he was no better than a simpleton." [11] Given a fairy story that starts this way, one can easily predict its ending: Jack the Fool will ultimately triumph, achieving what his elders have been unable to accomplish. And the same prediction can be made about Christy.

We are told that he has brothers and sisters, and that they have not been able to free themselves from their father, even after escaping from home and leaving Christy alone with old Mahon. "He'd sons and daughters walking all great states and territories of the world," Christy says, "and not a one of them, to this day, but would say their seven curses on him, and they rousing up to let a cough or sneeze, maybe, in the deadness of the night." They are not truly free, not free as Christy in the end is free: in the nights they wake to curse their father. It remains for Christy, the foolish son, to subdue the father once and for all.

The first "murder" is nearly an accident, and its maturing effects

[10] Joseph Jacobs, ed., *More Celtic Fairy Tales* (New York, 1895), p. 110.
[11] "Jack and His Master," Jacobs, *Celtic Fairy Tales,* p. 182.

are stumbled upon by accident. Christy strikes his father almost in self-defense, after an argument over whether he is to marry the rich old widow his father wants for him. He tells his story in the tavern largely because his pride is touched by the suggestion that he is wanted by the police for commonplace reasons. His true realization of what the murder means grows only gradually, fostered by the reactions of those to whom he tells his story. Soon, as a result of it, he comes to think of himself as, in effect, a poet: the equation between poetry and violence remains constant throughout the play. "I've heard all times it's the poets are your like," Pegeen says, "fine fiery fellows with great rages when their temper's roused." The image appeals to Christy, and becomes his picture of himself. To himself, to the rest of the world, he had hitherto seemed, in his own words, "a quiet, simple poor fellow with no man giving me heed." But now, to himself and to the rest of the world, he is a "fine fiery fellow"—a poet and a hero. Christy has apparently achieved freedom and power with the greatest ease: he remarks himself that he was a fool not to have killed his father long before. His new assurance carries him to triumph in the games even though his father has actually appeared before then: he relies on the Widow Quin to protect him, and assumes that people's belief in him as a father-murderer is as good as the reality.

But when Christy and his father are brought into conjunction, in the third act, it becomes immediately clear that manhood is not so easily won. The old man starts beating his son, and the passive Christy is reviled and ridiculed by all. His grandiose self-image is destroyed: he defends himself finally not on the basis of his achievement, but because he has never hurt anyone, except for his single blow. But the man of no violence, as Christy is soon brought to see, is no poet and no hero; he is the eternal victim, the scapegoat. Understanding for the first time what failure means, he can no longer accept it willingly. His rejection by the company makes Christy see that his earlier success has been an illusion, based, as he says, on "the power of a lie," and that he has substituted for loneliness the company of fools. Yet the effects of the first "murder" make the second one possible: Christy bolsters himself with the memory of his physical and rhetorical triumphs and, so strengthened, dashes out to kill his father again.

W. H. Auden has suggested that one of the distinguishing characteristics of the fairy tale is its stress on the power of the wish: the wish is the main cause of fairy tale events. "The cause of all wishes is the same," he writes—"that which is should not be. . . . When a scolded child says to a parent, 'I wish you were dead,' he does not mean what he actually says; he only means 'I wish I were not what I am, a child being scolded by you.' "[12] Christy's attempts to murder his father are fairy-tale-like enactments of such a wish: not so much that the old man should be dead as that he, Christy, should no longer be in a position to be humiliated by his father—and, by extension, humiliated by the rest of the world. But the second "murder" is different from the first. The first is a spontaneous reaction to humiliation; the second is a calculated and aware reaction. The wish has turned to will: Christy has perceived—or thinks he has perceived—that actual violence is necessary for social acceptance. And violence, after all, is still a simple matter. He has but to strike his father once again, and the impossible will be accomplished: Pegeen will be properly won, and Christy will be at last truly free.

The blow is struck, and Christy expects his reward, as the fairy tale hero after each trial is likely to think that trial the last. The Widow Quin warns him that he will be hanged, but he indignantly rejects the suggestion. "I'm thinking," he says, "from this out, Pegeen'll be giving me praises the same as in the hours gone by." And, a bit later: "I'm thinking of my luck to-day, for she will wed me surely, and I a proven hero in the end of all." But it is Pegeen herself who drops the rope over his head, Pegeen who calls his act "a dirty deed," Pegeen who burns his leg as he lies bound on the floor. For Pegeen and the others this "killing" has none of the symbolic richness of the "gallous story" Christy told of his first murder, the story which seemed to identify him as a man of great stature and great passions. The storyteller as hero is another familiar figure in Irish folk lore. In "Conal Yellowclaw," the hero wins freedom for his three doomed sons by telling three stories; "The Story-Teller at Fault" constructs an elaborate fiction around the dilemma of a storyteller with no tale to tell.[13] And

[12] W. H. Auden, "The Wish Game," *The New Yorker* (March 16, 1957), p. 134.
[13] Jacobs, *Celtic Fairy Tales*, pp. 34–46, 131–43.

Christy as man in action seems less heroic than Christy as story-teller. The second attack on his father has been too transparently motivated by the desire for approval; it is in no way heroic. Christy's mistake, however, is rectified as a result of the attack on him it causes. The first "murder" made the second one possible, in typical fairy tale fashion, and so does the second bring about the third. For as a result of being totally rejected by those who have previously praised him, Christy discovers for the first time that he doesn't *need* these fools.

The third "murder" takes place before our eyes, and is entirely verbal and symbolic in its enactment: Christy discovers he can give his father orders, shove him out the door, tell him that their relation now is to be that of "a gallant captain with his heathen slave." Having achieved, as a result of experience, genuine self-confidence, he can manage a real triumph, without violence, and one not based on a lie or motivated by desire for approval. Christy has yearned to escape the domination of his father and others; he fulfills his wish at last in appropriate terms, freeing himself not by physical murder, but by asserting his own power to dominate. The stupid son has become a hero, has inherited the kingdom and claimed his rights as ruler. If, contrary to the convention of the fairy tale, he does not win the princess, it is only because she is not worthy of him: he could have her now that he scorns her. It is Pegeen, indeed, who underscores his triumph, breaking into lamentations for her loss of one who, she realizes at last, is after all "the only Playboy of the Western World."

The word "playboy" is defined, in effect, by the action of the drama; it comes finally to mean the hero in the sense of a man who can "play" successfully with language, triumph in the "play" of athletic contests, excel in the "play" of flirtation and courtship. As he leaves the stage for the last time, Christy has become a playboy indeed, the man and the pose finally identical. And here the word "playboy" is used of him for the first time without ironic overtones. It has previously been employed to stress the disparity between Christy's pose and the actuality. The word is first spoken by Widow Quin, laughing at Christy, who has been huddled in terror behind the door while she talks with his father. She observes, "Well, you're the walking Playboy of the Western World, and that's the poor man you had divided to his breeches belt." The Widow Quin uses the word a second time in the context of Christy's victory in the games, still with the irony of her superior awareness. She tells old Mahon that the people are cheering "the champion Playboy of the Western World," and the old man is thereby led to think that this could not possibly be his worthless son. The fact that Christy's father is still alive is revealed to the crowd, and they jeer at the lad by calling out, "There's the playboy!" And when, in the curtain speech, Pegeen wails, "Oh my grief, I've lost him surely. I've lost the only Playboy of the Western World," the import of the phrase depends upon our knowledge of its previous ironic uses. Now at last it is spoken without irony, and now at last it *can* be applied without irony: Christy has won the right to the title.

Pegeen's final lamentations are preceded by her final rejection —with a box on the ear—of Shawn, her official suitor. Shawn, the true fool of the play, points up by contrast all the way through not only the superior richness of Christy's character, but the importance to that character of the father-murders. Father-destruction is, after all, an archetypal theme, and the primitive *necessity* of father-murder is stressed in *The Playboy* by the character of Shawn, who is totally unable to free himself from authority. He pleads for himself, in the second act, that he doesn't *have* a father to kill. But Shawn is clearly—and ridiculously—dominated by a father-figure, the priest, Father Reilly. When other characters in the play refer to Shawn, it is almost always in conjunction with Father Reilly; the lad is notoriously under the thumb of the priest, whose authority he is always citing, and of whom he is admittedly afraid. The priest is his excuse for lack of courage and imagination, for unwillingness to do the unexpected. None of his neighbors respect him; his subjection is too complete. Pegeen's father admits that he'd rather have Christy's children for grandsons than Shawn's, who would be only "puny weeds." The man who is dominated is a weakling; he must assert his individuality—must metaphorically kill his father—before he is to be respected. Both positively and negatively, then, the point is stressed. The idea of father-murder is the thematic center of the play, a center with precisely the sort of mythic overtones that are so often found in folk tales.

The ritual power of the "murders" in the play is reinforced by the ritual power of the language. Susanne Langer has suggested the essential similarity between the symbolism of metaphor and the symbolism of ritual; a sense of this intimate relation between language and ritual dominates *The Playboy of the Western World.* If it can be said that Christy is created as a man by his successive "murders" of his father, it can be said with equal truth that he is created by the force of language. The murder of his father represents, from the beginning, a sort of metaphor of achievement; Christy's verbal metaphors also define a pattern of achievement. Symbols are brought to life in this play in a rather special way. It has been commonplace, at least since Freud, that for primitive people the relation between word and thing is close, that the magic of spells depends upon the notion of this close tie. In *The Playboy* language seems to have power in the real world, as spells have power—as language in the folk tale has power. As Christy develops self-command, he develops also command of language; his increasingly poetic speech reflects his increasingly imaginative perception, and with the final subduing of his father comes a final control of language. Yet in another sense it might be said not that Christy comes to control language, but that language comes to control him.

The idea of himself as a poet, suggested by Pegeen, comes to have great importance for Christy; it is for him and the others inextricably connected with the idea of the hero. When the young man makes his first appearance, his speech has the strong folk rhythm of all the characters and some flashes of imagination, but he is essentially prosaic. Deciding to stay, he says, "It's a nice room, and if it's not humbugging me you are, I'm thinking that I'll surely stay." His reaction, in short, is that of the practical man—or the man trying to be practical. Left alone with Pegeen, after the suggestion that he is a poet has been made, he describes his father "going out into the yard as naked as an ash tree in the moon of May, and shying clods against the visage of the stars till he'd put the fear of death into the banbhs and the screeching sows." The father flings clods at the stars and gets a response from pigs; the disproportion between stimulus and response here suggested marks the situation of Christy himself, a dreamer by inclination whose life has hitherto been bounded by the most mundane details. Stars and moon are the typical material of his expanding metaphors. Pegeen, annoyed with him, seems to drive him away; as he goes to the door, he describes himself as "lonesome, I'm thinking, as the moon of dawn," and Pegeen is won to call him back. His metaphors grow more extravagant as his confidence develops. He speaks of Pegeen as having "the star of knowledge shining from her brow," and connects her repeatedly, in his references to her, with "the heavens above." In the wooing scene, he appeals to her with elaborate images of love-making beneath the moon and stars, and insists on the superiority of Pegeen to anything offered by the Christian heaven: he talks of "squeezing kisses on your puckered lips, till I'd feel a kind of pity for the Lord God in all ages sitting lonesome in his golden chair." Finally, at the height of Christy's first illusory triumph, Pegeen's father reports Father Reilly as saying that the dispensation has come in the nick of time, so he'll wed Pegeen and Shawn in a hurry, "dreading that young gaffer who'd capsize the stars." There has been no evidence that Father Reilly is an imaginative man; indeed, he seems to stand for all that is opposed to imagination. When he makes this comment about Christy, we feel as though the youth's most extreme metaphors have become fact, have formed the facts: as though it were indeed conceivable that Christy should overturn the stars, unlike his father, whose attempts at the stars only arouse the farm animals. Similarly, in a slightly earlier scene, old Mahon, not recognizing his son, comments, "Look at the mule he has, kicking the stars." Christy has somehow been created a true giant—and created partly by the power of his metaphors.

The same pattern of development from prose to extravagant poetry is repeated in miniature in the brief scene between Christy's humiliation by his father and his second murder attempt. It is repeated again, with a difference, between the second "murder" and the third. Once more, Christy's language develops in power as the lad develops in self-realization, but this time the self-realization is successful, and the language has an entirely new quality. No longer dependent on the opinion of others, Christy gains a new freedom; his speech, too, gains new freedom, a quality of pure joy different from anything it has had before. He talks of hell now as he had talked of heaven, but without the sense of unreality that clings to his earlier metaphors. The fusion of joy and reality that Synge spoke of as one of his goals in the play is complete at the very end. Christy leaves us with his vision of " a romping lifetime," couched in romping language.

So *The Playboy of the Western World* presents essentially the vision of a man constructing himself before our eyes. Not only does Christy construct himself: he creates his princess. Pegeen is, after all, a matter-of-fact girl with a hot temper. But she is not that sort of girl after a conversation with Christy. As Christy's images grow more and more compelling, Pegeen becomes more and more gentle and eloquent herself. She, too, seems to be changing before our eyes. Finally she comments on the phenomenon: "And to think it's me is talking sweetly, Christy Mahon, and I the fright of seven townlands for my biting tongue. Well, the heart's a wonder." But it seems to be the sheer power of language that has won Pegeen, and she apparently recognizes the fact herself when she says she'd not wed Shawn, "and he a middling kind of a scarecrow, with no savagery or fine words at all."

The importance of the idea of Christy as a constructed man is stressed by the fact that it is the main source of the play's humor as well as of its serious import. The comedy of *The Playboy* depends heavily on the ironic conjunctions between the felt ritual importance of the Playboy's role and the evidence of his incompetence or pettiness in the real world. The girls come to do him homage, bearing gifts, deducing from his boots that he is one who has traveled the world; they find him indulging in petty vanity with the looking glass. Christy describes himself as "a gallant orphan cleft his father with one blow to the breeches belt"; immediately afterwards he staggers back in terror at the sight of his living father. The young man is enjoying his triumph; his father comes in and starts beating him. Over and over the device is employed, to insist on Christy's efforts to make appearance and reality coincide, the name of hero correspond to the actuality. And as the central action of the ritual "murders" is reflected by the patterns of Christy's language, so the ironic conjunctions of the action are symbolized by such verbal patterns as the one we have noted around the word "playboy."

The sense of the fairy tale which one is likely to get from *The*

Playboy does after all, then, provide clues for a reading of the play which solves the problem of the relation between realism and fantasy in it, and also suggests the sources of its strange power. The themes, the language, the import of the play resemble those of folk tale and myth; its "serious" aspects and its comic ones alike, it seems, may be largely accounted for by this relation.

Synge's Playboy as Mock-Christ

by Howard D. Pearce

Even though critics frequently grant *Riders to the Sea* or *Deirdre of the Sorrows* to be the "greatest" of Synge's plays, *Playboy of the Western World* has for many the most hearty appeal of all. One may wonder, though, at reasons for such popularity in view of the profound gulf that separates the two most commonly held interpretations of the Playboy himself: on the one hand he is thought to become a hero in the final act, and on the other a mock-hero. I find little attempt among the critics to justify one view or the other, on the contrary the fundamental understanding of his character usually colors or generates a concept of the play. Alan Price, in the most thorough and recent study of Synge, thinks of Christy as a hero, seeing in this play, in contrast to *The Well of the Saints,* Synge's fusion of the "dream" and the "actuality," [1] watching Christy develop through the action "from weakling to hero." [2] Una Ellis-Fermor likewise sees him developing, "not merely into 'a likely man,' but into a poet-hero, 'the only playboy of the western world.' " [3] H. H. MacLean devotes an article to exploring Christy's Christ archetype, which makes of Christy a myth-generated hero.[4] I have severe doubts about rigorously applying archetypal patterns to the play, but it might be interesting to look at

"Synge's Playboy as Mock-Christ" by Howard D. Pearce. From Modern Drama, *VIII (December, 1965), 303–10.*

[1] Alan Price, *Synge and Anglo-Irish Drama* (London, 1961), p. 162.

[2] *Ibid.*, p. 178.

[3] Una Ellis-Fermor, *The Irish Dramatic Movement* (London, 1939), p. 177. [Reprinted above, pp. 35–48.]

[4] Hugh H. MacLean, "The Hero as Playboy *UKCR,* XXI (Fall, 1954), 9–19.

the Christ parallel again to see if Synge has not used the myth to ironic purposes not entirely consistent with MacLean's reading.

Even though it seems a minority voice, there certainly exists an ironic interpretation of Christy. Krause sees the "mock-heroic treatment of Christy" as deriving from the Ossian prototype.[5] He in addition finds in Synge a "counterpoint of idealism and irony," where "lyric and satiric modes are played against each other." Peacock in the same way proposes a far more subtle comprehension of Synge's vision in the play than that which makes Christy simply a hero:

> The basis of the comic here is a delicate and capricious mockery at the very idea of fine language, closely related as it is to fine ideas. Synge plays in this comedy with his own discovery. Through his mock-hero Christy Mahon he allows his instrument to elaborate its most splendid ornaments.[6]

Here, then, is an evasive hero whose similarities to Christ should perhaps be seen in the same light.

Christy Proteus-like shifts before our eyes, before his associates' eyes, and before his own. He has always tried to see himself, has not simply begun doing so when we catch him with the mirror at the beginning of Act II. Mahon deprecates his eternal romancing, including "making mugs at his own self in the bit of glass we had hung on the wall." [7] Where he has been seen a hero in general by the Mayo people, Mahon makes him a frightened rabbit, a "looney," which we of course suspected from our first glimpse. There is in the final action the obviously diametrical movement of Christy upward in the eyes of the audience and downward in the eyes of the Mayo people. Yet it is not an unqualified movement. The truth lies not in one pair of eyes, but in the reality of the contradictions that result from the shifting perspective. Surely the antithetical views achieved by Christy himself and Pegeen should leave the spectator a range in

[5] David Krause, "'The Rageous Ossean': Patron-hero of Synge and O'Casey," *MD,* IV (1961), p. 283.

[6] Ronald Peacock, *The Poet in the Theatre* (New York, 1946), p. 113. [Reprinted below, pp. 101–6.]

[7] John M. Synge, *The Complete Plays* (New York, 1960), p. 49. [Subsequent references to the plays are to this, the Vintage paperback edition.]

which to see the irony of Christy's self-glorification and Pegeen's disillusion.

One of the most fundamental ironies in the play rises from the apotheosis of an ostensible murderer. Christy's coming strikes fear into the hearts of the folk in the shebeen, especially Shawn, who has heard (or felt) him "groaning wicked like a maddening dog" in the ditch above. (p. 10) Yet when they have learned that he is a murderer, Pegeen is ready to take him as her defender for the night, and Philly and Jimmy reinforce her argument. (p. 19) They create of him a champion of discord and conflict. Killing his father is admired as an act of courage qualifying him as defender *against* the law and champion of gaming competition. When the Widow Quin first proposes him for the sports, Sara says, "I'll bet my dowry that he'll lick the world" (p. 34)—not that he will save it, but lick it. The Widow later applies to him the epithet "champion of the world." (p. 59) Mahon, of course, seeing him from a different angle considers him an anti-Christ. He asks, ". . . and isn't it by the like of you the sins of the whole world are committed?" (p. 73) Christy declares himself delighted with and devoted to his own evil at last, again a kind of anti-Christ. In the fracas of Act III, when Shawn thinks he will die from being bitten by Christy, Christy answers with delight, "You will then, the way you can shake out hell's flags of welcome for my coming in two weeks or three, for I'm thinking Satan hasn't many have killed their da in Kerry, and in Mayo too." (p. 79) The full force of the irony strikes in Michael's eloquent concession to Pegeen's avowed marriage to Christy instead of to Shawn. He joins their hands, pronouncing his blessing: "A daring fellow is the jewel of the world, and a man did split his father's middle with a single clout, should have the bravery of ten, so may God and Mary and St. Patrick bless you, and increase you from this mortal day." (p. 71) That baroque Christ-epithet "jewel of the world" is coupled with the grotesquely visualized "split his father's middle with a single clout," achieving the mockery of lyricism observed by Peacock.

A more comprehensive irony may be seen in that generally speaking Christy does offer a kind of salvation to his devotees. His power of romancing seems so much more finely tuned than theirs that he comes to embody the illusion which they try to turn to practicality. The Widow Quin's schemes show the severity and immediacy of her need for him as he is. When he romanticizes Pegeen, the Widow Quin says, "There's poetry talk for a girl you'd see itching and scratching, and she with a stale stink of poteen on her from selling in the shop." (p. 51) And though Pegeen can follow him in romantic flights, her hold on the illusion is so weak, so tentative, that it takes only one assertion by old Mahon to prove to her that Christy is a liar and "nothing at all." (p. 71)

We can see in terms of this dream Christy bears to them that in fact there is a ground for dramatic irony in his paralleling Christ. Where He was adored in His Epiphany, His people turned on Him at last and destroyed Him. For Christy, a lusty sex idol, the adoration of the Magi becomes the adoration of the local girls.[8] Christy thinks they trekked four miles to see him, until Pegeen informs him that they came no distance at all "over the river lepping the stones." (p. 39) The gifts they bear—"a brace of duck's eggs," "a pat of butter," "a little cut of cake," and "a little laying pullet" (p. 34) —effectively parody the gifts of the Magi. Sara even teases Christy about his divinity, asking, when he will not use his right hand to touch the gifts, "Is your right hand too sacred for to use at all?" (p. 34) The betrayal comes, of course, when the people lose their illusion and become again fearful of the law.

Certainly, as MacLean argues, this betrayal turns Christy into a mythic scapegoat figure.[9] He comes to them as sufferer, Pegeen asking, "Aren't you destroyed walking with your feet in bleeding blisters, and your whole skin needing washing like a Wicklow sheep." (p. 20) But after his moment of glory with them they reject him when Mahon turns up alive and threatening vengeance on Christy —first Pegeen, then all. He turns at last to the Widow Quin, who declares that her "share is done," (p. 73) then to the others, and Sara mocks him with advice to turn to Pegeen again. After he has again "killed" his father, they do not merely reject, but set about destroying him to protect themselves. Michael says, "If we took pity

[8] MacLean (p. 14) notices this incident, but to make it fit his scheme terms it a "temptation" merely, eschewing the obvious parallel of the girls to the Magi.

[9] MacLean, p. 9.

on you, the Lord God would, maybe, bring us ruin from the law today," (p. 77) and Pegeen echoes him with "take him on from this, or the lot of us will be likely put on trial for his deed today."

Around this scapegoat idea plays the theme of mock-sacrifice which illuminates a serious depth in the play. A good bit of "saving" goes on in the play, but far earlier and more frequently not "saving" but bribery. Both of these grow from the essential selfishness of human nature seen in the various reasons for accepting Christy in the first place: Pegeen likes and wants him, Michael wants to get out of the house, Philly thinks he will keep the peelers away. Christy reveals his father's secret motive in trying to marry him to the Widow Casey, ". . . letting on I was wanting a protector from the harshness of the world, and he without a thought the whole while but how he'd have her hut to live in and her gold to drink." (p. 36) Further, much of the plot turns upon bribery. Mahon will tell Philly and Jimmy of his "murder" if they will give him a supeen. (p. 56) Shawn tires to bribe Christy to go away, (p. 44) and when that fails tries to bribe the Widow Quin, who skillfully turns the affair into, not bribery, but sacrifice. He asks what she will do if he promises her a ewe, she answering, "A ewe's a small thing, but what would you give me if I did wed him and did save you so?" (p. 45) The Widow Quin offers the same kinds of bribes to lure Christy away from Pegeen—not wealth but leisure, since Christy is such a lazy fellow (p. 52)—but when he in turn asks the Widow to help him win Pegeen, to "aid and save [him] for the love of Christ," (p. 53) she again agrees for the payment of "a right of way . . . , a mountainy ram . . . , and a load of dung at Michaelmas."

Yet the Widow Quin's mock-sacrifice takes a strange turn in the final action. The Widow seems all along one who has been almost entirely free of illusions about Christy. She admires him less for the lie than for the reality—he is a handsome lad. Thus it is not surprising that when the illusion dies she does not betray him. (Admittedly, Sara leagues with the Widow, but her admiration for Christy seems, like the Widow's, less dependent on his story than on his face.) Of course it is Christy's father who finally "saves" him from the avengers—the so-called "savior" is at last saved. But the Widow, aided by Sara, tries to save him as well. Seemingly her motives are still practical and selfish, but on the other hand she appears poignantly aware of that Syngean vision of the mutability of youth and beauty, trying to save him not merely for herself, but because it would be a shame for him to die. She offers him finer sweethearts than Pegeen, again bribing him away, then, when he refuses to give up the illusion and takes a stool to them all, she goes out saying to Sara, "It's in the mad-house they should put him, not in jail, at all. We'll go by the back-door, to call the doctor, and we'll save him so." (p. 76) If Widow Quin lacks the sparkle and romance of Christy, nevertheless her actions, grounded in actuality, in such sharp contrast to Christy's, which are irremediably floating in the dream vision, point up Synge's ironic detachment. His impetus arises not merely from love or hate, resulting in neither simply romance nor bitter satire, but some complex interrelationship of the two.

This view of Synge is necessary in order to avoid oversimplifying his characters and as a result the entire play. In suggesting that those parallels with the Christ myth illuminate the play, my purpose is to show Christy as a mock-Christ, a mock-hero. We see facets in this way which cannot be seen from one perspective. If we take his recognition in the last scene as a simple thing, then we are led to oversimplify Synge's vision. Certainly he admired the rambunctious self-assurance and glamor Christy has put on in espousing the dream. But I think that, especially through such elements as the implicit grace of Widow Quin's final action, it is obvious that Synge saw Christy's affirmation as no absolute answer to the conflict. Price seems to come dangerously near such an oversimplification in his assertion of the paradox that the dream becomes the actuality.[10] The matter is not simply Pegeen's inability to grasp the dream. The sad truth is that the dream and the actuality remain as disparate here as in *Deirdre of the Sorrows.*

Christy comes into this Western World an innocent and a romancer, and he goes out of it the same, influenced by that world primarily to self-confident braggadocio. It may be that he loses innocence, but even here the conversion seems only partial. He shows a naiveté early in the play which makes him kin to such other characters as the Tramp in *In the Shadow of the Glen.* Christy is, of

[10] Price, p. 162.

course, like the Tramp in that they share the romantic vision and are wanderers and free men,[11] but they are further alike in having a kind of innocence that leaves them astounded by and vulnerable to the shocks they receive from other men. The Tramp is unbelieving when Dan would put Nora out of the house: "It's a hard thing you're saying for an old man, master of the house, and what would the like of her do if you put her out on the roads?" (p. 115) When Dan shows himself adamant, the Tramp suggests that Michael Dara might then take her, an idea absurd to all the realists, for she now has no dowry to offer Michael. (p. 116) Christy, too, only with difficulty understands the viciousness of mankind. In Act II, when Pegeen has tormented him with the story of the hanging (which is her way of repaying him for accepting naively and promiscuously the attentions of other females), he complains, "What joy would they have to bring hanging to the likes of me?" (p. 40) He is no more knowledgeable about man's laws than about those "queer joys" (p. 40) which make men torment others. In recounting his past adventures in proaching, he says, "I was a devil to poach, God forgive me, (*very naïvely*) and I near got six months for going with a dung fork and stabbing a fish." (p. 24) His innocence of females is the source of much humor in the play, of course, Mahon revealing his being the butt of jokes and having the title "the looney of Mahon's." (p. 49) And he does not give up this innocence easily. Even after Pegeen's complete rejection of him, he still expects her to relent, (p. 75) accepting the truth only after she says that she will burn him. (p. 78)

Corollary to this innocence is his utter romanticism. Mahon declares him "a liar on walls, a talker of folly, a man you'd see stretched the half of the day in the brown ferns with his belly to the sun." (p. 48) He romanticizes Pegeen and himself, even innocently supposes that he has found a pastoral idyll among the good people of Mayo. (p. 22) The romancing, of course, grows beyond proportion, until he imagines in the last scene his own hanging: ". . . the day I'm stretched upon the rope with ladies in their silks and satins snivelling in their lacy kerchiefs, and they rhyming

[11] Herbert Howarth, in *The Irish Writers 1880–1940* (London, 1958), p. 226, affirms the paradox of the wanderer and the "rooted man" in Synge's own personality.

songs and ballads on the terror of my fate." (p. 78) This declaration far better shows the ridiculous lining of his romanticism than does the frequently quoted line about "romancing through a romping lifetime." (p. 80)

I asserted above that Christy only partially loses his innocence and naiveté. This can be seen in the quality of his "tragic recognition." Far from arriving at some deeper truth, he gains a superficial self-assurance without the more profound understanding which would accompany a tragic hero's "reversal." His final affirmation is on a grand scale, but it remains grand comedy, a mockery of Maurya's acceptance, Deirdre's heroic passion, and Nora's pathetic realization of the imperfection in the Tramp's promise of life. What Christy specifically learns is that Mayo is not the fulfillment of his dream. He came thinking the promise of peace which Pegeen offered him (p. 26) was attainable, thinking that "You're decent people . . . and yourself a kindly woman." (p. 22) He thought he had found perfection on earth, ". . . a clean bed and soft with it, and it's great luck and company I've won me in the end of time," (p. 30) ". . . a fine place to be my whole life talking out with swearing Christians . . . , smoking my pipe and drinking my fill, and never a day's work." (p. 31) Nature is idyllic still in the duet of love he and Pegeen sing in Act III. (pp. 64–66)

But he had known all along the imperfection of the people of Clare: "Oh, they're bloody liars in the naked parish where I grew a man," (p. 22) as he had known of the bleakness of nature, the "cold, sloping, stony, divil's patch of a field" (p. 35) where he killed his "da." Thus what he learns when Pegeen deserts him and the crowd cheers Mahon against him is that people are fools, (p. 74) an opinion echoed by Mahon as they go off together: ". . . my son and myself will be going our own way, and we'll have great times from this out telling stories of the villainy of Mayo, and the fools is here." (p. 80) Christy has realized merely that the people of Mayo are no better than those of Clare, that he has not found the dream. But he goes on naively seeking the dream, with no sounder justification for the search nor any improved chance of finding it. His new daring holds little promise of changing the world or the people in it.

Yet there is joy in his affirmation. We applaud his act of domination, perhaps for the comic justice in it, the underdog's winning the day, perhaps for the gusto itself. It is ironic that our sympathy has grown for Christy not because of his pride, domination, and rejection of the world, but for the opposite: his pathetic need to find a place in it. Christy before his triumph often seems to come close to the perception of Nora, who in accepting the Tramp's offer recognizes the stark reality of her action: "I'm thinking it's myself will be wheezing that time with lying down under the Heavens when the night is cold; but you've a fine bit of talk, stranger, and it's with yourself I'll go." (p. 118) Christy's speech, ". . . it's a lonesome thing to be passing small towns with the lights shining sideways when the night is down . . ." (p. 41) is now famous. The sadness which is part of the wanderer's lot is not unknown to him —all the more ironic his exuberant blindness in the end, thinking that lot is nothing but joy. Before the reversal, the lonesomeness of the Widow Quin causes him to see, "You're like me, so." (p. 52) Then as he faces his rebelling devotees, he bares the horns of the dilemma of human existence with the pathetic realization that ". . . you're setting me now to think if it's a poor thing to be lonesome, it's worse maybe to go mixing with the fools of the earth." (p. 74) (His is essentially the plight of Huck Finn, who comes up with a similar, and no better, solution to this conflict.) One may have love, escaping loneliness, or one may have freedom, escaping the evils bred in man, but he may not have both. He may flee, and thus dominate, or succumb, but not both. Christy has here stated the dilemma but has remained blind, or perhaps grown even blinder, to the loss involved in making a choice, a loss which Synge shows a full awareness of in his other plays.

Thus even though Christy is made into a deity, the apotheosis contains ironies. Since he comes as a Christ-destroyer, rather than saying he in fact in actuality destroys, overpowers, "licks" his people (with words, at least, though obviously he is instrumental in Pegeen's destruction) instead of sacrificially succumbing to their destroying him. As he grows to a heroic affirmation, there remains mockery implicit in the disparity between the grandeur of it and the degree of ignorance that engenders it. The danger is that the spectator may be taken in by the apotheosis as the good people of Mayo were by the Epiphany. To avoid becoming subject to the simple assertion of this hero, one must maintain a finely turned ear for the lyric and the mockery of it, the heroic and the mock-heroic, and the discrepancy between the actuality and the dream.

PART THREE

View Points

David H. Greene: The Composition of *The Playboy*

A small notebook which Synge used during the Aran period contains a short sketch of a play called "The Murderer," described in Synge's handwriting as a farce. The entire sketch and the bits of dialogue with it constitute the earliest attempt at what later became the *Playboy.*

> Act I (a potato garden). Old Flaherty describes his son's life and exasperates him so much that in the end he takes the loy and hits his father on the head with it then runs across the stage and out on left.
>
> Act II (Public house, Bar or Shebeen). Christy bossing the show, tells his story three times of how he killed his father. Police are afraid to follow him and other bombast, love affairs, etc. At the slightest provocation he starts off again with his story.
>
> Act. III. He is being elected county councilor. Old man comes in first and shows his head to everybody. He is as proud of it as his son is, as he is going round the crowd. His son comes out the elected member. He is put on a table to make a speech. He gets to the point where he is telling how he killed his father when the old man walks out. "You're a bloody liar, that's what you are."

The pages of the book were torn out at this point, but the fragments that are left amount to about forty pages of dialogue. This sketch is probably the basis of Yeats' remark that "Synge gave up his intention of showing upon the stage a fight in a ploughed field between the Playboy and his father. . . ."

There is little in this very early sketch and the pages of dialogue accompanying it to throw much light on how the play evolved, but the main elements are there. The manuscripts which were found

---

"The Composition of The Playboy*" by David H. Greene. (Title supplied by the editor.) From "*The Playboy *and Irish Nationalism,"* Journal of English and Germanic Philology, *XLVI (April, 1947), 200–202. Reprinted by permission of the publisher, University of Illinois Press.*

after the author's death, however, (they include 7 complete versions of act 1, 8 of act 2, and 10 of act 3) show how Synge filled out his conception of characters and plot until they reached final form. First he gave up the idea of the election motif and substituted the romance with Pegeen as the central theme. He developed Shawn Keogh, a minor character, into a rival for Christy. Next, he decided to rehabilitate the character of Christy after the parental exposure. In the earlier versions Christy is dismissed as a coward when his irate father shows up very much alive; he walks off tamely and the play ends with a street singer shown composing a ballad on the whole subject.

> Young Christopher the daddy man came walking from Tralee
> And his father's ghost the while did keep him company.

When Shawn Keogh tells him to stop his singing, that the murder was a fake, he rings down the curtain with,

> Oh, God help me and I after spending the half of me day making of his deed. But it's a lovely song. Well I'll sing it other roads where he's not known at all. It's a lovely song surely.

One early version has the renunciation scene taking place before the door of the chapel, with the old man getting there just in the nick of time to prevent the marriage of Christy and Pegeen. Lady Gregory, who apparently saw this version because she mentions it, may have had something to do with Synge's discarding the idea.

The verbal revisions which intervened between the original draft and the final version show that Synge's main endeavors were first to tone down the vulgarities, which he is known to have loved, and second to develop the rhythm of the lines so that content and mood would be unified by the sound of the dialogue. The two objectives must frequently have conflicted, because some of the most explosive and rhythmic phrasing of the earlier readings is diluted into respectable but stolid mediocrities. For the most part, however, the moderations consist of such changes as "belching ass" to "Kerry mule," Old Mahon "stinking" in his obscure grave to "lies rotting in his obscure grave." It is hair-raising to think of how the indignant audiences would have received the deleted phrase of one of the early drafts which reads, "To hell with the Pope."

But most of the verbal revisions consist of skillful maneuvering of words and phrases purely for rhythmic effect. Synge filled the margins of the early drafts with self-instructions to improve the sound. Two examples will suffice to show how he worked out some of his effects and succeeded in writing some of the finest prose-poetry of the modern theater.

In an earlier reading of act three Christy imagines himself looking at Pegeen stretched back in the flowers of the earth, "the way I've heard the holy prophets stretching out their necks upon the wall of Heaven to look upon the lady Helen does be passing back and forward with a nosegay in her shawl." The "necks upon the wall of Heaven" becomes "their heads upon the bars of Paradise." Then *heads* and *necks* both give way to, "do stretch the bars of paradise and they striving to set their eyes on the Lady Helen abroad does her paces back and forward with a nosegay in her shawl." Not satisfied with the ring of it yet he adds, "If the mitred bishops would see you that time they'd be the like of the holy prophets," etc. Then *stretching* the bars of paradise gives way to *straining* the bars of paradise, and finally the passage reads:

> If the mitred bishops seen you that time, they'd be the like of the holy prophets, I'm thinking, do be straining the bars of Paradise to lay eyes on the Lady Helen of Troy, and she abroad, pacing back and forward, with a nosegay in her golden shawl.

A more remarkable example of his careful jockeying about of words is in the opening lines of act one. As the curtain goes up the publican's daughter is shown writing aloud. In the very first draft of the play the speech reads:

> Two dozens of Powers Whiskey. Three barrels of porter, two bottles of hops. To be sent by Timmy Farrel's creel-cart on the evening of the coming fair to Mister Michael James Flaherty. With the best compliments of this season. Margaret Flaherty.

The latter part of the speech strikes the right note at the very start; but the first part is all wrong because the three items she is ordering, the whiskey, porter, and bottles of hops, are short and jumpy and delay the lyric take-off which follows with "To be sent by Timmy Farrel's creel-cart. . . ." So in the margin Synge had written, "Try making her order her trousseau." On the back of the page is an attempt at the trousseau: "Six yards of yellow silk ribbon, a pair of long boots, bright hat suited for a young woman on her wedding day, a fine tooth comb to be sent. . . . The *long boots* he changes then to "pair of shoes with English heels," but still isn't satisfied, so he crosses out *English* and substitutes in succession the words *big, long,* and *lengthy*. The passage finally reads:

> Six yards of stuff for to make a yellow gown. A pair of lace boots with lengthy heels on them and brassy eyes. A hat is suited for a wedding-day. A fine tooth comb. To be sent with three barrels of porter in Jimmy Farrel's creel cart on the evening of the coming Fair to Mister Michael James Flaherty.

This kind of careful revision, which is evident throughout the whole play, shows verbal workmanship of a very high order and explains why the demands were so great on the actors for sound reading and sensitive delivery. Willie Fay, the first director of the Abbey Theater, remarks on the difficulties of mastering the rhythm of Synge's lines. "They had what I call a balance of their own and went with a kind of lilt."

Ronald Peacock: Synge's Idiom

The exotic appeal of Synge's work can scarcely be exaggerated; and it is another aspect of his romantic and lyrical character. I think there can be no doubt that Synge himself experienced the language and life he found in the Aran Islands as something rare and strange, beautiful because it was unsophisticated, remote, elemental. It awoke the artist in him, as Paris had not been able to do, because he was a romantic. And in this Synge is the pure artist, without any admixture of the political intentions that have always to be reckoned with in Yeats and other adherents of the Celtic renaissance. Yeats it was who sent Synge out to the West, helping a genius to find his line,

---

"Synge's Idiom" by Ronald Peacock. (Title supplied by the editor.) From The Poet in the Theatre, *2nd ed. (New York: Hill & Wang, Inc., 1960), pp. 110–15.*

but also making a démarche in the political cause of Irish nationalism. It is clear that Synge was independent of causes; an unpolitical artist, whatever use others made of his work once it was done. His pleasure in observing his primitives and in savouring their musical and picturesque language was from any point of view but the artistic irresponsible and non-commital. The storm about *The Playboy of the Western World* arose because there were many Irishmen who could not emulate such detachment.

As far as the Anglo-Saxons are concerned, I think Max Beerbohm came nearest to the truth when he stressed the exotic as the source of our greatest pleasure in Synge. It is, however, a judgement that has been obscured by more frequent tributes to his pure dramatic genius. No one would deny his natural sense of drama and theatre, his powers in comedy and tragedy. If he were without them his more personal charms would be thin and vapid perhaps. But he did not possess those powers in an astonishing degree, and they alone certainly do not make the Synge to whom we are endeared. They are the excellent soil above which the rare bloom raises its head. Synge's greatest distinction, the thing that gives our acquaintance with him its particular flavour, is his wonderful language, which pleases us not as a heightened form of the language we ourselves use, but as a picturesque deviation from it. Two things support each other; the setting of Irish character, atmosphere and speech is itself exotically attractive, and it is made more so, pointedly so, by Synge's exquisite and subtle handling of the imaginative peasant language he discovered in the West.

This view, with its emphasis on the pleasure we get from unfamiliar forms of life and language, runs counter to a simple appraisal of Synge's style as a great creation. It is "poetic" only within certain well-defined limits. It is very closely related to folk art and suffers from the same disadvantages. The "folk" imagination is spontaneous and beautiful as far as it goes; it does not always go very far. The simplicity and freshness and immediacy, the innocent and natural tones of folk art are not enough for mature phases of art. The influence of folk-song in German poetry, for instance, was beneficial in some ways, equally harmful, however, in others, for the reversion to its forms in the romantic era—after Goethe had outgrown them—retarded for nearly a century the development of new and more varied forms. Synge's language, for all its delicate modelling, loses in the long run by its limitation as folk-speech. In his slender production it suffices to express a rather narrow range of peasant character and simple feeling. Its style is all on the surface. It has not that expressiveness of great dramatic poetry that lies in its profound relevance to the underlying pattern of our own lives. Such language might be gorgeously metaphorical, as in Shakespeare, it might be eloquent, precise, intense, as in Racine, but it is anything but unfamiliar. Using the elements of our own language it completes and illuminates what we experience in an obtuse way. Judged by this proper standard, Synge's style is severely restricted. Where purer effects of dramatic poetry are required, as in *Deirdre of the Sorrows* —the one play whose subject-matter lies outside the range of his original discovery—his language in some passages even fails outright. Its picturesque or homely remoteness, so much a concomitant of its "poetic" appearance, obstructs the true effect of dramatic poetry. It diverts the attention to the surface instead of holding it upon the situation.

How much the idiom in itself has to do with Synge's art emerges from *The Playboy of the Western World.* The direct sensuous consciousness of a patently picturesque speech and way of thinking is the inspiration of this play; and the point gains in importance when we consider that this is his most ambitious work. The basis of the comic here is a delicate and capricious mockery at the very idea of fine language, closely related as it is to fine ideas. Synge plays in this comedy with his own discovery. Through his mock-hero Christy Mahon he allows his instrument to elaborate its most splendid ornaments. Some have been so entranced as to take it at its high face-value as sheer poetry. Yet it is the most precise exaggeration, a distillation of his own speech-material conceived in a vein of irony. Christy Mahon is a wonder to the people of Mayo and he talks himself into a wonder for his own imagination. Their reactions are focused in him. The figurative phrases that pour from his lips are his own beautiful amplification of *their* response to the lad he was, of their fancy for the stupendous notion that he had killed his da. Fine words argue the fine idea, the alert imagination. The people who play up Christy are quick in esthetic reaction; for the sake of a fine story they instantly suspend their moral judgment. Synge brings them back to it:

> *Pegeen.* I'll say a strange man is a marvel, with his mighty talk; but what's a squabble in your backyard, and the blow of a loy, have taught me that there's a great gap between a gallous story and a dirty deed.

It has been pointed out how Synge got the germ of this drama from an old man on Inismaan. His use of what he was told points in the direction of the argument we are putting forward. He heard how a man who killed his father was protected by the islanders until he could be got off to America. Synge comments:

> This impulse to protect the criminal is universal in the West. It seems partly due to the association between justice and the hated English jurisdiction, but more directly to the primitive feeling of these people, who are never criminals yet always capable of crime, that a man will not do wrong unless he is under the influence of a passion which is as irresponsible as a storm on the sea. If a man has killed his father, and is already sick and broken with remorse, they can see no reason why he should be dragged away and killed by the law.
>
> Such a man, they say, will be quiet all the rest of his life, and if you suggest that punishment is needed as an example, they ask, "Would anyone kill his father if he was able to help it?"

Synge has so transformed both the initial situation and the attitude of his characters to the doer and his deed that it is almost true to say he owes nothing to the story told him. He discards the event in its original form and substitutes a pure fantasy. And he quite changes the motives of the peasants. The mixed impulse of pity and charity and obscure reverence which made them help the unfortunate parricide he replaces by a gay and reckless love of a marvel told, and told marvellously.

Surprisingly enough, Synge's delicate self-mockery in *The Playboy of the Western World* leads us back in a roundabout way to the esthetic cults of the *fin de siècle.* Synge immersed himself in a local material—men with sharp profiles, living a hard and lowly life—and he has given such a vivid picture of them, that his physical severance from Paris and its artistic currents seems at first sight to have its complete counterpart in his work. But looking below the surface of these *genre* pictures, of this apparently impersonal drama, one discovers other things. This comedy is not directed only against the people of Mayo, but against Synge himself; against the artist and his dangerous love of fine words. It is at once the fullest display—conscious display—of his most distinguishing gift, and an ironic commentary on it. The love of fine words for their own sake, symbolized in Christy Mahon at its intensest though in a comic inversion, is a form of the search for something ethereal and esthetically refined, some musical quintessence. It was very original of Synge to discover this in a milieu that was in no way artificial or recherché or ultrasophisticated; nevertheless it shows him in closer relation to some literary tendencies of the atmosphere he deserted than is generally supposed. Synge's work is most praised amongst that of his contemporaries for its imaginative quality; it is less often noticed that his most ambitious work has for its very theme the imagination, the fine idea and the fine word. From this point of view it is one of those works, often of dubious inspiration, in which the artist takes art and artists for his subject. It is, however, wonderfully disguised; and the disguise—the comedy and the irony—gives it its quality.

Viewing Synge in some of the ways I have tried to indicate means modifying a little our more excessive tributes of praise. His real achievement is that he went his own way when almost everyone else in drama was fanatically social and "contemporary," and he found something akin to the poetic in an out-of-the-way place, with the result that his work goes on living with the life of imaginative creations when those who imagined themselves to be so intensely "alive" are dead. And yet from the point of view of the English drama during his lifetime and since, his work has been singularly unhelpful, however fine the figure he makes. For the drama wanted at that time two things: a poetic form and a contemporary consciousness. The latter it had in a crude way; the former it lacked entirely. With Synge the position was reversed. His consciousness was nineteenth-century and romantic; he looked backward, not forward. On the other hand, he had, within the limits we have indicated, a style, but one that was quite useless for the

English drama, its basis being a speech of extremely local and ambiguously English character. He is therefore without influence on English dramatists.

Herbert Howarth: The Realist Basis of Surreality

[Synge] has offered brief definitions of his aesthetic in his prefaces. But the prefaces are so deliberate, lapidary, that we cannot make much of them. Just a phrase or two can usefully be examined for his intentions, notably the remark in the preface to *The Playboy*: "On the stage one must have reality, and one must have joy." Shall we read this as "reality . . . and *therefore* joy" or "reality . . . and *yet nevertheless* joy"? Given the state of Ireland, Synge must have meant the latter. He did combine reality and joy, or at any rate reality and exhilaration, and knew that he had accomplished a paradox. His immediate seniors had not been able to do it, nor even to conceive of it. When AE first saw the Congested Districts in the west, he was horrified to silence; in 1897, when he had just begun his rural tours for Plunkett, he wrote to Synge from Belmullet in Mayo: "This wild country here has imposed such a melancholy into my blood that I have not had the heart to write to [Yeats] or anybody else if I could help it. I had nothing to say except accounts of the distress here which is a disgrace to humanity and that is not cheerful subject matter for a letter." [1] Synge was just as aware of the distress of the Districts when he travelled them with Jack Yeats in 1905, and his prose studies contain the dour reality. But he reared *The Playboy* around the villainy of the men of Mayo, and set it not far from Belmullet; and in the play there is no reality in the English novelist's sense of the term, no fact documented and evaluated; there is Synge's kind of reality.

Some critics might judge the word "reality" inapplicable to his drama. There is an obvious sense in which he invests Mayo

---

"The Realist Basis of Surreality" by Herbert Howarth. From The Irish Writers 1880–1940 *(London: Barrie & Rockliff, 1958), pp. 220–25. © 1958 by Herbert Howarth. Reprinted by permission of Hill and Wang, Inc., and Barrie & Rockliff.*

[1] *Letters from AE,* edited by Alan Denson.

or the Wicklow glens with a vigour which is the antithesis of the drab reality and a compensation for it. Yeats thought so in the summer of 1904 when, writing from Coole where he, AE, and Synge were guests of Lady Gregory, he described Irish plays as "a cry for a more abundant and a more intense life." [2] Synge doubled reality into surreality, giving Ireland what she lacked as well as what she showed him. But he did include what she actually showed together with what he imagined for her. His dialogue supplies images of aspirations, couched in what an Egyptian friend of mine used to call "hashish-poetry," and images drawn from harsh fact. It is a direct counterpoising of reality and dream. Christy's famous speech which uses the conventional Gaelic love-image of "the star of knowledge" turns on the contrast of aspiration, in which the Church and the body are confused, and penurious fact:

> Amn't I after seeing the love-light of the star of knowledge shining from her brow, and hearing words would put you thinking on the holy Brigid speaking to the infant saints, and now she'll be turning again, and speaking hard words to me, like an old woman with a spavindy ass she'd have, urging on a hill.

and Widow Quin's retort caps the reality:

> There's poetry talk for a girl you'd see itching and scratching, and she with a stale stink of poteen on her from selling in the shop.

—an Irish portrait that looks forward to Molly Bloom. Synge disperses what we usually imagine as beauty and in its place finds energy. Energy is the quality that we finally count as beauty in him. Yeats wrote of Synge's "harsh, heroical, windswept view of things," and of those three adjectives the most characteristic is "windswept," suggested by Synge's own description of the exhilarating open and the wind in his teeth like wine. The sensation of Synge *is* harsh and it *is* exhilarating; it is impossible to live long with it, and yet we tell ourselves under its shock that our nerves are so alight that we are living as never otherwise, lifted out of

[2] But see the whole of this interesting letter in Allan Wade's edition of *The Letters of W. B. Yeats,* p. 436.

torpor. The shortness of Synge's life was the registration of this difficulty in his kind of beauty.

Christy's exchange with Widow Quin is relatively simple, and often in Synge the pattern of hope against fact is more intricate, an interfluxion of the real and the surreal, a dependence of the real on the surreal to retain vision and energy, and a dependence of the surreal on the real for efficacy; and the real and the surreal operate as drama—not merely as art which happens to be written in dialogue—because the real elements in the combination necessarily predicate stage-business or inflections of the voice. Synge had learned in Aran that a drowned, headless man may be identified by his clothing. Nora in *Riders to the Sea* identifies her brother by counting the stitches in his stocking: "It's the second one of the third pair I knitted, and I put up three-score stitches and I dropped four of them." Her sister counts the stitches to check her. The epic quality has this commonplace domestic reality at its centre; and the conception is a stage-conception; the actresses must play to each other handling the stocking. In the wonderful sequence of smelling the boot in *The Playboy* Synge exploits domestic reality, requires the third dimension of the group-handling of an object, and enhances the tang of the grotesque vital to his best work. The second act opens with the girls of the locality rushing into the shebeen to find Christy. Sara Tansey picks up his boots:

> *Nelly*. Are you thinking them's his boots?
>
> *Sara* (*taking them up*). If they are, there should be his father's track on them. Did you never read in the papers the way murdered men do bleed and drip?
>
> *Susan*. Is that blood there, Sara Tansey?
>
> *Sara* (*smelling it*). That's bog water, I'm thinking.

This is one of the two dozen masterly stage-strokes in *The Playboy*. It is at once social realism and farce; it belongs to the special Irish family of olfactory comedy, that extravagant distillation of the unwashed; it is essentially conceived as drama, notates the actresses' business, and requires them to perform as well as speak the combined realism, poetry, lowness, exaltation.

Of course, the recognition of the stitches in *Riders* is neither so rich nor so impure as that *Playboy* episode. It is the realism of compassion, and there are other similar moments in Synge. When Mary Byrne at the close of Act I of *The Tinker's Wedding* says "It's few would listen to an old woman, few but a girl maybe would be in great fear the time her hour was come, or a little child wouldn't be sleeping with the hunger on a cold night," she offers in the last image simply the poverty of Ireland. But in *The Playboy,* which has had such success that the critics like to look elsewhere to praise Synge, for fear of the obvious, but which is his consummate work, the norm is the heterogeneous. A hard compassion goes together with hyperbole, which is a grand exotic flowering, like Christy's account of his father: "he after drinking for weeks, rising up in the red dawn, or before it maybe, and going out into the yard as naked as an ash tree in the moon of May." This is a visualisation of the father as god and object of worship, not formed through a realistic comparison but carved archetypally out of the unconscious by a man who grew up never knowing his father. Breaking momentarily out of the give-and-take of the real and unreal in Synge's special way it is superb. The extravagances are safely anchored in the reality with which they are associated.

The Playboy was denounced by Dublin for its theme of parricide, but the fact is that, while it makes its comedy from audacious, close looks at the Oedipean struggle between father and son, it ends with father and son united. It is a play of the discovery of the unknown father, a father different from the clerkly, studious, charitable men Synge's immediate begetters seem to have been, a figure outwardly stingy and gigantically repressive, but lit at the centre by rough family love. Christy's early speeches show his fear and anger with his father, but the inner warmth. He answers Michael James when he is asked whether the police want him for larceny:

> *Christy* (*with a flash of family pride*). And I the son of a strong farmer (*with a sudden qualm*), God rest his soul . . .

Just as the movement of Synge's ideas entails stage-business, so it impels the actor to effective shifts of voice. The break in that sentence of Christy's notates a gasp of recollection, a modulation from pride which is nearly but unconsciously love, to remorse which brings love nearer to consciousness.

The dynamic conceiving of speech and action in terms of the performer is common to every able dramatist (though there are not over many of these at the poetic level). But how did Synge acquire it? Shakespeare had to write more than five plays before he acquired it. We first hear Shakespeare notating for voice and action originally, poetically, and with a clarity the actor may not disregard, in *Romeo and Juliet*; it is an inferior play in thought, but it has that special interest in the Shakespearian canon, that the dramatist is, after some practice, suddenly in control of his medium. Synge had the control before he had any professional practice. Certainly he had the advantage of writing with 300 years of British drama behind him, and of careful study of some of the English and French standard plays both in his room and among theatre audiences, and perhaps he had observed experimental plays on the stage in Middle Europe; he is said to have been taken, like Joyce, by Ben Jonson's comedy; but all this is not an explanation, for hundreds of us have read Jonson and Molière without assimilating a single trick. When he actually worked with the players he probably improved his sense of the trade, as Lady Gregory gained hers; but he had written *The Shadow* and *Riders* before that. Nothing could be a simpler trick, but nothing apter or better-handled, than the sequence in Dan Burke's kitchen when Nora, who believes her husband to be dead under the sheet behind her, talks to her lover about him, and the audience sees him rising to the very posture she is describing: ". . . It's a queer thing to see an old man sitting up there in his bed with no teeth in him, and a rough word in his mouth, and his chin the way it would take the bark from the edge of an oak board you'd have building a door. . . ." Synge meditated three-dimensionally. Most word-markers meditate in the one dimension of the rhythm, they incantate; a few can alternatively, and fewer still can also, meditate in the second dimension of the verbal image; but to be capable of these and the third dimension of action, which sometimes runs with and sometimes contrapuntally against, the verbal image, is reserved for the rare born dramatist. Apply this test to Eliot, and, for all his fine accomplishment in the theatre, he is not a born dramatist; he has only the first two dimensions. Synge was. "How" remains a mystery of family genetics (since he grew out of clergymen—but there is admittedly a connection between the church service and the drama) and of national genetics (since he grew up in a country that never had a native drama).

We are occasionally told that Synge was a master of construction. It is true that his structures are excellent, especially in that they do not proclaim their excellence. But they are not intricate. Synge knew what he could do and did not attempt more. With appropriateness and clarity he placed a few effects where they could not fail.

J. L. Styan: On Playing with the Audience

The Playboy of the Western World is good drama for this reason, that the plot is simplicity itself, but nevertheless the response of the audience is subtle and delicate and of considerable complexity. In urging this it has the economy of great playwriting. It is an amalgam of ironies, and the complexity of the audience's response is due to the way in which the author manages with the visual and aural detail of his dialogue to flex and vary and refine our impressions. The meaning of the scene is intenser, its outline sharper, its importance greater, although by comparison the narrative action on the stage is bald. Thus the triple twist to the tail of the play is not a perversity, but a natural outcome of a play which is a mosaic of twists.

The first act carefully sets the tone and drift of the ironies. From Christy Mahon's first entrance, the stage presents a pattern of fluctuations in the tempo and movement of the characters as they veer between doubt of and respect for Christy. At first those in the shebeen patronize him:

> *Pegeen.* There's a queer lad. Were you never slapped in school, young fellow, that you don't know the name of your deed?

"On Playing with the Audience" by J. L. Styan. (Title supplied by the editor.) From The Elements of Drama *(Cambridge, England: Cambridge University Press, 1963), pp. 57–63. Reprinted by permission of Cambridge University Press.*

Their interest in the crime increases rapidly upon Christy's "I'm not calling to mind any person, gentle, simple, judge or jury, did the like of me," to the crisis, "Don't strike me. I killed my poor father, Tuesday was a week, for doing the like of that." On this admission they retreat from him in some respect. But it remains a doubtful respect until they hear the manner of the crime: "I just riz the loy and let fall the edge of it on the ridge of his skull." From here Christy's confidence begins to grow with their esteem.

This is a severe summary of the line of the action, but it shows how the audience's regard for Christy will contrast with Pegeen's and Michael's, Philly's and Jimmy's. The life of the whole play is in that contrast. Our attitude to him was in part determined by his bathetic entrance:

> *For a perceptible moment they watch the door with curiosity. Some one coughs outside. Then Christy Mahon, a slight young man, comes in very tired and frightened and dirty.*
> *Christy in a small voice.* God save all here!

The first impression of his slightness is the foundation of the spectator's estimation of him. Interest in Christy will grow as the characters' interest grows, but the nature of our response will differ in inverse proportion. When they glorify Christy

> *Philly.* There's a daring fellow.
> *Jimmy.* Oh, glory be to God!

our instinct is to vilify him. We do not do this because, of course, we do not readily jump to conclusions when a scene is still in progress. We are more bothered by the difference between our reaction to Christy and that of the characters. Christy is the focus of attention for the characters on the stage, but the spectator's attention embraces the whole stage picture.

Having thus prepared his audience, Synge goes on to sharpen the impression with this:

> *Pegeen.* That'd be a lad with the sense of Solomon to have for a pot-boy, Michael James, if it's the truth you're seeking one at all.
> *Philly.* The peelers is fearing him, and if you'd that lad in the house there isn't one of them would come smelling around if the dogs itself were lapping poteen from the dung-pit of the yard.

Jimmy. Bravery's a treasure in a lonesome place, and a lad would kill his father, I'm thinking, would face a foxy divil with a pitchpike on the flags of hell.

Pegeen. It's the truth they're saying, and if I'd that lad in the house, I wouldn't be fearing the loosed khaki cut-throats, or the walking dead.

Christy, swelling with surprise and triumph. Well, glory be to God!

Michael, with deference. Would you think well to stop here and be pot-boy, mister honey, if we gave you good wages, and didn't destroy you with the weight of work?

Shawn, coming forward uneasily. That'd be a queer kind to bring into a decent, quiet household with the like of Pegeen Mike.

Pegeen, very sharply. Will you whisht? Who's speaking to you?

Shawn, retreating. A bloody-handed murderer the like of . . .

Pegeen, snapping at him. Whisht, I am saying; we'll take no fooling from your like at all. *To Christy with a honeyed voice.* And you, young fellow, you'd have a right to stop, I'm thinking, for we'd do our all and utmost to content your needs.[1]

The question arising in the discussion is, Will a murderer make a good pot-boy?—one grotesquerie among the many that compose the fabric of the play. All the characters except Shawn are trying to persuade Michael to employ the stranger; superficially, therefore, we get an accumulation of arguments for it. Christy is reluctant to say where he killed his father, so Pegeen attributes to him "the sense of Solomon." The peelers have not followed him, so Philly twice suggests they "is fearing him, and if you'd that lad in the house there isn't one of them would come smelling around." And finally, to complete this trio of advisers, Jimmy points out that killing one's father takes bravery, so it is argued that Christy is brave, and "Bravery's a treasure in a lonesome place." We are not intended to feel incongruity between the three speeches, since they are in accord. Irony does not arise therefore by any comparison between what they say. But each echoes the illogicality of the other, the folly of the reasoning in each case making the total argument more and more ridiculous, especially as each contributor raises his voice a tone higher and speaks with increasingly assertive Irishisms. We are being asked to believe by implication that a

[1] Synge, *The Playboy of the Western World,* Act I.

killer would be just the one to have in a lonesome place with you, that black is white, that two and two make five. There is irony in the wit here of course, and we laugh at the incongruity of it, but such irony and such laughter are of the surface only.

The real incongruity, the real irony and the real control over the spectator springs from their *agreement*. We would have expected Philly to contradict Pegeen, Jimmy to contradict Philly, and finally we would have expected Pegeen to stop the progress of an argument moving so quickly towards the ludicrous. Instead she pursues it with a note of flirtatiousness in her voice and manner. Pegeen the single girl, Pegeen who will have to work with him, live in the house with him, caps them both with, "if I'd that lad in the house, I wouldn't be fearing the loosed khaki cut-throats, or the walking dead." She would prefer Christy to a Tommy and to a spectre; if she had with her a killer with a loy, she would not fear a killer with a knife; if she had with her a man whose conscience was burdened by the ghost of a dead father, she would not fear a ghost itself. Impression A does not confound impression B: it underlines it, and underlines impressions C and D as well. Our imagination is daringly distorted. The spectator asks himself what statement Synge is making, what to believe. Because there is a strict antithesis between our logic and theirs, and because they are thinking in unison, we can only deduce by our standard of behaviour that they are mad, the more so for appearing so serious in what passes for their reasoning. We bridge the theatrical gap between our minds and theirs with a mental gesture of half-dismissal: we laugh. But now Synge can weave his bizarre magic on us.

Christy is surprised too: "Well, glory be to God!" So they are not all in a conspiracy of madness, and their response was not wholly to be expected after all. Perhaps our first impression of Christy as rather a contemptible young man was a right one: Christy's remark evidently confirms us in this. But the attention of Pegeen, Philly and Jimmy has been directed on Michael, and now our attention is led there too. Michael will surely resolve the contradiction. We wait in the slight pause, savouring the situation and trying the weight of Michael's decision. We anticipate something like "The saints forbid that ever I should do the like of that!" but instead we hear a gentle, deferential voice: "Would you think well to stop here and be pot-boy, mister honey. . . . ?" And Michael goes on to offer good wages and light work. The gap is strained again. We are not certain what to think. Is impression A in relation to impression B unmeaning? Is our recognition of a criminal, supported as it is by a code of right and wrong, to have no support from the characters on the stage and to bear no relation to any code of values within the play? We are left wondering again at the characters' irrational behaviour. Perhaps we are to dismiss it as we dismiss it in farce? But the stage action as it has been described is not complete.

Our critical response is not allowed to be so simple, because Shawn is on stage too, cowering in the corner, and, observe, reacting to Christy in a manner quite different from the others. Synge has been at pains through the first ten minutes of the act to fill out the character of Shawn. He is not there simply to contrast with Christy. He is there in chief to establish and show the conventional response to a murderer and a patricide. Is it then intended that he should be our chorus, and as *raisonneur* represent our feelings towards Christy? No, for how could this be? His is an excessive physical cowardice and a fanatical and hyper-religious attitude. We must be reluctant to let this sort of example be our guide: "God help me, he's following me now, and if he's heard what I said, he'll be having my life, and I going home lonesome in the darkness of the night."

Yet it is Shawn who now speaks our *own* comment: "That'd be a queer kind to bring into a decent, quiet household." Was it accident that we phrased the comment we anticipated from Michael as Shawn would have spoken it? So Synge judges us, and uses Pegeen, who was earlier taking her death with the fear, to reprove Shawn and us: "we'll take no fooling from your like at all." We observe she says "we," and draws together the majority against Shawn. By the movement of her body and the change in her tone, she isolates him, the outsider, one not in the compact. And she reduces his eminent reasonableness to "fooling." But who is fooling?

We are left undecided, our attitude unsettled, with no certain finger left us to wag, our received impression askew. But we are forced to reconcile and make shapely this grotesquerie if we are to sit comfortably through the play. If we choose to accept Synge's coloured view of his Irish peasant characters, and can stomach this extraordinary method of revealing it to us, the play will supply a nice insight into human nature. We may even care to echo what Mr Edmund Wilson said in 1931, that this was the most authentic poetic drama the century had seen.[2] If not, we may boo with the first audiences who saw it at the Abbey Theatre in 1907. There are not many plays in which the author is so playful with his audience, or juggles with its feelings and adjusts the focus of its imagination so sportively to achieve his ends. *The Playboy* is a bold use of the theatre, and a good example of how extravagant a dramatist can be.

[2] E. Wilson, *Axel's Castle* (1931), p. 43.

Chronology of Important Dates

	Synge	*Historical and Cultural Events*
1871	J. M. Synge born, April 16, at Rathfarnham, near Dublin.	Franco-Prussian War ends.
1872	Death of Synge's father.	
1891		Death of Parnell. Theatre d'Art founded. First performances of Ibsen's *Hedda Gabler,* Maeterlinck's *The Intruder.*
1892	Graduates from Trinity College.	Yeats's *The Countess Cathleen* published. First performance of Hauptmann's *The Weavers.*
1893	Leaves for Germany to study music.	
1895	Leaves for Paris to study languages and literature.	First performance of Wilde's *The Importance of Being Earnest.*
1896	Meets Yeats in Paris.	First performance of Chekhov's *The Sea Gull.*
1898	First of five visits to the Aran Islands.	The People's (later, Moscow) Art Theatre founded. Rostand's *Cyrano de Bergerac* published.
1899		Irish Literary Theatre founded. Boer War (to 1902).
1902	Returns from Paris to Dublin.	First performances of Yeats's *Cathleen ni Houlihan,* Gorki's *The Lower Depths.* Lady Gregory's *Cuchulain of Muirthemne* published.

1903	First performance of *In the Shadow of the Glen.*	Shaw's *Man and Superman* published.
1904	First performance of *Riders to the Sea.*	Abbey Theatre founded. First performances of Lady Gregory's *Spreading the News,* Shaw's *John Bull's Other Island.*
1905	First performance of *The Well of the Saints.*	Russian Revolution of 1905.
1906	Becomes engaged to Molly Allgood.	
1907	First performance of *The Playboy of the Western World. The Aran Islands* published.	First performance of Strindberg's *A Dream Play.* Joyce's *Chamber Music* published.
1908	*The Tinker's Wedding* published. Death of Synge's mother.	First performance of Strindberg's *The Ghost Sonata.*
1909	Synge dies, March 24, in Dublin. *Poems and Translations* published.	
1910	First performance of *Deirdre of the Sorrows. The Works of John M. Synge* published.	Death of Edward VII.

Notes on the Editor and Contributors

THOMAS R. WHITAKER teaches at the University of Iowa. He is the author of *Swan and Shadow: Yeats's Dialogue with History* and *William Carlos Williams.*

WILLIAM BUTLER YEATS (1865–1939)—the great Irish poet, playwright, and man of letters—was a founder and a director of the Abbey Theatre.

UNA ELLIS-FERMOR (1894–1958) taught for many years at the University of London. Her books include *Christopher Marlowe, The Jacobean Drama, The Frontiers of Drama,* and *The Irish Dramatic Movement.*

CYRIL CUSACK, the noted actor and director, worked with the Abbey Theatre from 1932 to 1945 and then formed his own company at the Gaiety Theatre in Dublin. His production of *The Playboy* (with himself as Christy and Siobhán McKenna as Pegeen) was recorded in 1955 (Angel Album 3547-B).

T. R. HENN teaches at St. Catharine's College, Cambridge University. His books include *Longinus and English Criticism, The Lonely Tower,* and *The Harvest of Tragedy.*

NORMAN PODHORETZ edits *Commentary.* He is the author of *Doings and Undoings: The Fifties and After in American Writing* and *Making It.*

PATRICIA MEYER SPACKS teaches at Wellesley College. She has written books on eighteenth-century poetry—*The Varied God, The Insistence of Horror, John Gay,* and *The Poetry of Vision*—and articles on modern drama.

HOWARD D. PEARCE teaches at Florida Atlantic University. He has published articles on Herman Melville, Walt Whitman, and Maxwell Anderson.

DAVID H. GREENE teaches at New York University. He is the author of *J. M. Synge 1871–1909* (with Edward M. Stephens) and has edited *1000 Years of Irish Prose* (with Vivian Mercier) and *Fingal Rónáin and Other Stories.*

Ronald Peacock teaches at Bedford College, the University of London. His books include *The Poet in the Theatre, The Art of the Drama,* and *Goethe's Major Plays.*

Herbert Howarth teaches at the University of Pennsylvania. He is the author of *The Irish Writers 1880–1940* and *Notes on Some Figures Behind T. S. Eliot.*

J. L. Styan has taught at the University of Hull and the University of Michigan. His books include *The Elements of Drama, The Dark Comedy,* and *Shakespeare's Stagecraft.*

Selected Bibliography

The definitive edition is J. M. Synge, *Collected Works,* ed. Robin Skelton (London: Oxford University Press). This includes: *Poems* (I), ed. Skelton (1962); *Prose* (II), ed. Alan Price (1966); and *Plays* (III-IV), ed. Ann Saddlemyer (1968). Ann Saddlemyer's introduction to Volume IV describes the writing of *The Playboy* and interprets the riots; the notes and an appendix include material from Synge's draft manuscripts, related passages from his prose works, and his published defences of the play.

Readers may also find the following works useful:

Bourgeois, Maurice. *John Millington Synge and the Irish Theatre.* London: Constable & Co. Ltd., 1913. The most thorough of the early studies, with data on first performances, translations, early criticism.

Gerstenberger, Donna. *John Millington Synge.* New York: Twayne Publishers, Inc., 1964. Contains an assessment of *The Playboy* as drama of a young poet's self-discovery.

Greene, David H., and Edward M. Stephens. *J. M. Synge, 1871–1909.* New York: The Macmillan Company, 1959. The official biography, which includes much that is relevant to the writing of *The Playboy* and its first production.

Gregory, Lady Augusta. *Our Irish Theatre.* New York: G. P. Putnam's Sons, 1913. Comment on her association with Synge and on the controversies over *The Playboy.*

Johnston, Denis. *John Millington Synge.* New York: Columbia University Press, 1965. An introductory essay by an Irish playwright of the following generation.

Price, Alan. *Synge and Anglo-Irish Drama.* London: Methuen & Co. Ltd.,

1961. Includes a detailed analysis of *The Playboy* as dramatizing the fusion of "dream" and "actuality."

Saddlemyer, Ann. " 'A Share in the Dignity of the World': J. M. Synge's Aesthetic Theory," in Robin Skelton and Ann Saddlemyer, eds., *The World of W. B. Yeats*. Rev. Ed. Seattle: University of Washington Press, 1967, pp. 207–19. A study of Synge's explicit theorizing.

TWENTIETH CENTURY INTERPRETATIONS

Maynard Mack, *Series Editor*
Yale University

NOW AVAILABLE
Collections of Critical Essays
ON

Adventures of Huckleberry Finn
All for Love
Arrowsmith
As You Like It
Bleak House
The Book of Job
The Castle
Doctor Faustus
Dubliners
The Duchess of Malfi
Euripides' Alcestis
The Frogs
Gray's Elegy
The Great Gatsby
Gulliver's Travels
Hamlet
Henry IV, Part Two
Henry V
The Iceman Cometh
Julius Caesar
Keats's Odes

Oedipus Rex
The Old Man and the Sea
Pamela
The Playboy of the Western World
The Portrait of a Lady
A Portrait of the Artist as a Young Man
The Rime of the Ancient Mariner
Samson Agonistes
The Scarlet Letter
Sir Gawain and the Green Knight
The Sound and the Fury
The Tempest
Tom Jones
Twelfth Night
Utopia
Walden
The Waste Land
Wuthering Heights